Praise for

PROJECT TO PRODUCT

With the introduction of the Flow Framework, Mik has provided a missing element to any large-scale Agile transformation. I recommend that anyone involved in complex product delivery read this book and think about how they can apply this thinking to their value stream.

—**Dave West**, CEO Scrum.org and author of *Nexus Framework for Scaling Scrum: Continuously Delivering an Integrated Product with Multiple Scrum Teams*

During our transformation to "100% Agile" BMW Group IT organization, we discovered early on that the former project portfolio approach did not sufficiently support our journey. Therefore, we started with a transition from "project to product." The exchanges with Mik on the topic of product orientation and the Flow Framework was very helpful and a real inspiration for me. The fact that Mik is now sharing his vast knowledge in this book makes me particularly happy. It provides the motivation and the toolset necessary to help create a product portfolio based on a value driven approach. For me it is a must read—and indeed it is also a fun read.

—**Ralf Waltram**, Head of IT Systems Research & Development, BMW Group

Organizing software development as a group of loosely connected projects will never lead to good products. Kersten explains how to tie work products to value streams corresponding to features, defects, security, and (technical) debt.... [*Project to Product* is a] major contribution to the theory of management in the age of software.

—**Carliss Y. Baldwin**, William L. White Professor of Business Administration at the Harvard Business School, Emerita, and co-author of *Design Rules, Volume 1: The Power of Modularity*

If you want to get rid of obsolete practices and succeed with the new digital, read this book.

—**Carlota Perez**, author of *Technological Revolutions and Financial Capital: The Dynamics of Bubbles and Golden Ages*

Every now and then, a body of work comes along with such timely precision that you think hallelujah! Mik's book *Project to Product* is the perfect antidote for those businesses struggling with digital transformation, broken Agile implementations, and the onslaught of enterprise disruption. In fact, it's really important component in the world of flow which is at the forefront of business agility. Not only will this framework help your teams to ignite their software delivery cadence but to do it at scale with high quality, reduced costs, and increased value. And more importantly, with happy teams—and with the metrics to prove it.

—**Fin Goulding**, International CIO at Aviva and co-author of *Flow: A Handbook for Change-Makers, Mavericks, Innovation Activists, Leaders: Digital Transformation Simplified,* and *12 Steps to Flow: The New Framework for Business Agility*

I had the pleasure of having an advance copy of *Project to Product* at my company over the summer—and what an eye opener it is. This book is spot on the journey Volvo Car Group is starting up right now. The insight Mik has in our industry and the way his book describes the Age of Software makes this our new "go to" book for our product journey in our digital landscape!

—**Niclas Ericsson**, Senior IT Manager, Volvo Car Corp

Project to Product is going to be one of the most influential reads of 2019 and beyond. One that connects work outcomes to business results. One that provides models to make better business decisions. One that gives technology leaders a framework to enable the change necessary for companies to remain relevant.

—**Dominica DeGrandis**, author of *Making Work Visible: Exposing Time Theft to Optimize Work & Flow*

Many large organizations are still applying a management model from the early 1900s optimized for manual labor to everything they do, including complex, unique, product development. With this book, Mik provides a great articulation of the importance of focussing on the work not the workers, on the value stream network, and lessons learned on what to avoid. Mik, who has many years experience working with hundreds of companies on this topic, shares his wisdom and insights via a Flow Framework, which is immensely valuable for organizations who recognize the need to move to better ways of working.

—**Jonathan Smart**, Head of Ways of Working, Barclays

Project to Product is a very insightful book, and the overall model Mik lays out for the Flow Framework is especially intriguing. Not only does Mik address the complexities of Agile transformation and moving to a product-based development, he also discusses how to get your architecture, process, and metrics integrated in a way to effectively measure value delivery. I got pretty excited about the Flow Framework and look forward to applying it to my own technology transformation activities.

—**Ross Clanton**, Executive Director, Technology Modernization, Verizon

PROJECT TO
PRODUCT
MIK KERSTEN

25 NW 23rd Pl, Suite 6314
Portland, OR 97210

First Edition
Printed in the United States of America

22 21 20 19 18   1 2 3 4 5 6

Cover illustration by Rachel Masterson
Figure illustrations by Zhen Wang
Cover and book design by Devon Smith
Author photograph by Janine Coney

Library of Congress Catalog-in-Publication Data
is available upon request.

ISBN: 978-1-942-78839-3
eBook ISBN: 978-1-942-78840-9
Kindle ISBN: 978-1-942-78841-6
Web PDF ISBN: 978-1-942-78842-3

For information about special discounts for bulk purchases or for information on booking authors
for an event, please visit our website at ITRevolution.com.

PROJECT TO PRODUCT

PROJECT TO PRODUCT

TO

HOW TO SURVIVE AND THRIVE IN THE AGE OF DIGITAL DISRUPTION WITH THE FLOW FRAMEWORK

MIK KERSTEN

FOREWORD BY
GENE KIM

IT Revolution
Portland, Oregon

To my mother, who made me who I am,
and my father, who taught me who to be.

CONTENTS

ILLUSTRATIONS

TABLES

FOREWORD

by Gene Kim

The mark of a great book is that it makes obvious what is wrong with the old worldview and replaces it with one that is simultaneously simpler and yet presents a better model of reality. The transition from Copernican to Newtonian physics has been long held as a great example of such a breakthrough. I believe *Project to Product* presents a new way to think that enables a new way of doing.

In today's business landscape, with companies facing the threat of digital disruption, the old ways of planning and executing no longer seem enough to survive. For decades, great minds have been seeking a way to manage technology to achieve business goals—after all, we know there is something very, very wrong with the way we're managing technology, we see the poor outcomes with our own eyes.

Project to Product makes the solid case that in the Age of Software, the methods that served us well for over a century are truly coming to an end: project management, managing technology as a cost center, traditional outsourcing strategies, and relying on software architecture as the primary means to increase developer productivity. And better yet, it provides a wonderful framework to replace it, namely the Flow Framework.

You'll learn what it looked like when an organization spent over a billion dollars on a technology transformation that was doomed to fail from the beginning because it was trying to solve the wrong problem. You will learn how some of the fastest growing companies nearly died by ignoring technical debt that was accumulated in their need to cut corners to ship products quickly, which included Nokia's massive Agile transformation that did nothing to stop its demise.

Dr. Mik Kersten brings the perspective of someone who got his PhD in software engineering only to discover that the massive productivity gains were not to be found there. Instead, those productivity gains can only be reaped when we change how teams across the entire business value stream work together, an epiphany common to so many of us in the DevOps community.

But he also brings the perspective of someone who built the large open-source software community around Mylyn in the Eclipse ecosystem, used by millions of Java developers. As founder and CEO of a software company, he brings a visceral understanding of what it's like to live and die by the ability of business, product, and engineering leadership to work together effectively.

You'll also follow in Dr. Kersten's professional journey and relive his three biggest epiphanies—fans of The Phoenix Project will especially love the lessons learned from the BMW Group Leipzig manufacturing plant, which he rightly calls "a pinnacle of the Age of Mass Production," and the profound lessons that the software industry can learn from it.

Project to Product is an incredible achievement. Dr. Kersten provides a better way to think about how business and technology organizations create value together, and provides the Flow Framework as a way for those leaders to plan and execute together, to innovate for their customers, and to win in the marketplace. To disrupt, instead of being disrupted. The upcoming Deployment Period Age of Software may bring the equivalent of an economic extinction event, so these capabilities are no longer optional for survival.

Every decade, there are a couple of books that genuinely change my worldview. You can tell which books they are, because more than one-third of the pages are bookmarked, indicating something I felt was truly an important a-ha moment or a reminder to myself to study further later. This is one such book.

I hope you find it as rewarding and life-changing as I did.

Gene Kim
Portland, OR
September 4, 2018

INTRODUCTION

The Turning Point

For the majority of our careers, those of us involved with enterprise IT have been dealing with change at a frenzied pace. Technology platforms, software development methodologies, and the vendor landscape have been shifting at a rate that few organizations have been able to match. Those that manage to keep up, such as Amazon, and Alibaba, are further driving change by redefining the technology landscape around their software platforms, causing the rest to fall even further behind.

This daunting and unrelenting pace of change has been seen as a hallmark of the digital disruption. But if we step back and look at the patterns of progress that came before, we begin to see ripples of the great surges of change and development of previous industrial and technological revolutions.

Over the course of three centuries, a pattern emerges. Starting with the Industrial Revolution, every fifty years or so a new technological wave combines with ecosystems of innovation and financing to transform the world economy.[1] Each of these technological waves has redefined the means of production so fundamentally that it triggered an explosion of new businesses followed by the mass extinction of those businesses that thrived in the culmination of the previous surge. Each wave has been triggered by the critical factor of production becoming cheap. New infrastructure is then built while financial capital drives the ecosystem of entrepreneurs and innovators who leverage the new techonological systems to disrupt and displace the incumbents of the last age.

Each of these technological revolutions has required existing businesses to master a new means for production, such as steam or the assembly line. For the digital revolution, the new means of production is software. If your organization has already mastered software delivery at scale, this book is not for you. The goal of this book is to provide everyone else with a new managerial framework that catalyzes the transition to the Age of Software.

Theories that explain the cycles of the last four technological revolutions and the first half of this one are proposed by Carlota Perez in *Technological Revolutions and Financial Capital: The Dynamics of Bubbles and Golden Ages* and by Chris Freeman and Francisco Louçã in *As Time Goes By: From the Industrial Revolutions to the Information Revolution*. Perez expands on the "long wave" or Kondratiev economic model by specifying two distinct periods within each cycle (Figure 0.1). The first half is the *Installation Period*, when a new technology and financial capital combine to create a "Cambrian explosion" of startups, disrupting entire industries of the previous age. At the end of the Installation Period is the *Deployment Period* of technological diffusion, when the production capital of new industrial giants starts taking over. Between these two periods is what Perez termed the *Turning Point*, historically marked by financial crashes and recoveries. This is when businesses either master the new means of production or decline and become relics of the last age.[2]

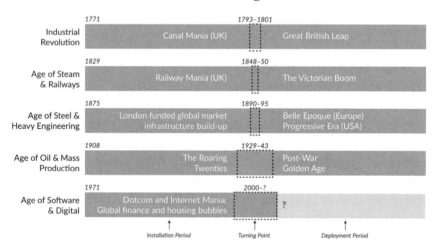

Figure 0.1: Technological Revolutions and the Age of Software.[3]

Fifty years have passed since NATO held the first conference on software engineering in 1968 and the Age of Software officially began. Today, the pace of change feels relentless because we are passing through the Turning Point. At the current rate of disruption and decline, half of S&P 500 companies will be replaced in the next ten years.[4]

These businesses, many of which were founded prior to the Age of Software, are starting to see a growing portion of their spending shift to technology as their market success is increasingly determined by software. However, the productivity of software delivery at enterprise organizations falls woefully behind that of the tech giants, and the digital transformations that should be turning the tide are failing to deliver business results.

The problem is not with our organizations realizing that they need to transform; the problem is that organizations are using managerial frameworks and infrastructure models from past revolutions to manage their businesses in this one. Managerial accounting, organizational hierarchies, and Lean manufacturing were critical to success in previous revolutions. But these managerial frameworks are no longer sufficient to successfully direct and protect a business in the Age of Software.

I had a chance to witness the pitfalls of this trap firsthand. Working with Nokia, I noticed that management was measuring the success of its digital transformation by how many people were trained on Agile software development methodologies and were onboarded onto Agile tools. These activity-based proxy metrics had nothing to do with business outcomes. As I will summarize in Part I, Nokia's transformation efforts failed to address the core platform problems that made it so difficult for the company to adapt to the changing market. In spite of what appeared to be a well-planned transformation, management was not able to realize this until too late. I watched with frustration as Nokia lost the mobile market it had created, in spite of the heroic efforts of my colleagues, who were doing everything they could to save the company.

A few years later, I was invited to speak with IT leaders at a global bank. The bank was six months into its third attempt at a digital transformation, and this time, DevOps tools were added to the mix and expected to save the day. The budget for the transformation was approximately $1 billion, but shockingly, I realized their transformation plan was even more flawed in its approach than the one at Nokia. Every aspect of the transformation was being project managed to cost reduction alone and not to project overall business outcome with reduced cost as a key metric. As I learned more, I started getting a visceral image that a billion dollars of the world's wealth was going to go up in flames without producing any value. There were still eighteen months left to right the ship, but I knew that with cost alone as the foundation of the transformation, it was too late to alter course. Nokia had left me with an image of a burning mobile platform that destroyed a tremendous amount of wealth and prosperity. I now had a vivid image of the bank's digital transformation lighting fires of waste across its ranks.

That was the day I started this book. There was something so fundamentally wrong with the way business people and technologists worked and communicated that even leaders with the best of intentions could still lead their companies into predictable decline.

How is this possible when we now have five decades of software practice behind us? The Agile and DevOps movements have made great strides in adapting key production techniques from the Age of Mass Production to the technical practice of building software. For example, continuous delivery pipelines allow organizations to leverage the best practices of automated production lines. Agile techniques capture some of the best technical management practices of Lean manufacturing and adapt them to software delivery.

The problem is, with the exception of some tech giants run by former software engineers, these techniques are completely disconnected from the way that the business is managed, budgeted, and planned. Software delivery concepts near and dear to technologists, such as technical debt and story points, are meaningless to most business leaders who manage IT initiatives as projects and measure them by whether they are on time and on budget. Project-oriented management frameworks work well for creating bridges and data centers, but they are woefully inadequate for surviving the Turning Point of the Age of Software.

In this book, we will examine several digital transformation failures that caused organizations to lose their place in the market. We will then dig further into understanding the current state of enterprise software delivery by looking at a study I conducted with Tasktop, "Mining the Ground Truth of Enterprise Toolchains," that analyzed the Agile and DevOps toolchains of 308 organizations to uncover the causes of this disconnect between business and technology.[5] *Project to Product* will then provide you with a new management framework and infrastructure model, called the Flow Framework, for bridging this gap between business and technology.

The Flow Framework is a new way of seeing and measuring delivery and aligning all of your IT investments according to value streams that define the set of activities for bringing business value to the market, via software products or software as a service (SaaS). The Flow Framework displaces project-oriented management, cost center budgeting, and organizational charts as the primary methods of measuring software initiatives. These are replaced with flow metrics for connecting technology investment to business results. The Flow Framework allows you to scale the Three Ways of DevOps—flow, feedback, and continual learning (as outlined in *The DevOps Handbook: How to Create World-Class Agility, Reliability, and Security in Technology Organizations*[6])—beyond your technology organization and to your entire business.

With each technological revolution, a new kind of infrastructure has been established in order to support the new means of production. Canals, railways, electrical grids, and assembly lines were key infrastructure components that underpinned the technological ecosystems of previous cycles. Many digital transformations have gone wrong by over applying infrastructure concepts of the last revolution to this one. Production and assembly lines are great at reducing variability and reliably producing similar widgets, but software delivery is an inherently variable and creative endeavor that spans a complex network of people, processes, and tools. Unlike manufacturing, in modern software delivery the product development and design process are completely intertwined with the manufacturing process of software releases. Attempting to manage software delivery the way we manage production lines is another instance where frameworks from previous technological revolution are failing us in this one. The Flow Framework points to a new and better way.

What if we could see the flow of business value within our organizations in real time, all the way from strategic initiative to running software, the way the masters of the last age ensured they could see and collect telemetry for every step of the assembly line? Would we see a linear flow or a complex network of dependencies and feedback loops? As the data set of 308 enterprise IT toolchains we will examine in Chapter 8 demonstrates, we see the latter. This flow of business value within and across organizations is the *Value Stream Network*. In the Age of Software, Value Stream Networks are the new infrastructure for innovation. A connected Value Stream Network will allow you to measure, in real time, all software delivery investments and activities, and it will allow you to connect those flow metrics to business outcomes. It will empower your teams to do what they love doing, which is to deliver value for their particular specialty in the value stream.

A developer's primary function and expertise is coding, yet studies summarized in this book have shown that developers spend more than half their time on manual processes due to disconnects in the Value Stream Network. These disconnects are the result of relics that go back two technological revolutions: Taylorism, which resulted in the treatment of workers as cogs in a machine,[7] and the silos that have formed in functionally structured organizations.

Successful businesses in the Age of Mass Production aligned their organizations to the value streams that delivered products to their customers instead of constraining themselves to rigid functional silos that disconnected specialists from each other and from the business. For example, Boeing, a master of the Age of Mass Production, could never have brought the highly innovative 787 Dreamliner to market and scaled its production to meet the growth in demand if the company had been structured like today's enterprise IT organizations. Organizations that manage IT delivery as projects instead of products are using managerial principles from two ages ago and cannot expect those approaches to be adequate for succeeding in this one. Visionary organizations are creating and managing their Value Stream Networks and product portfolios in order to leapfrog their competition in the Age of Software.

The future of software delivery is already here; it's just not evenly distributed yet. Software startups and digital natives have already created fully connected Value Stream Networks that are aligned to their product delivery, are focused on flow over siloed specialization, and connect all of their software delivery activities to measurable business results. Their leaders speak the language of developers, often because they were developers, which enables them to effectively direct their software strategies. What does that mean for the fate of every other company? How can we bridge the gap between technology and business leadership to create a common language that allows the rest of the world's organizations to thrive in the Age of Software?

While organizations ponder these questions, the tech giants that have mastered software at scale are expanding into traditional business, such as finance and the automotive industry. The tech giants are mastering traditional businesses more quickly than the world's established companies are mastering software delivery. In doing so, they're amassing a growing portion of the world's wealth and technology infrastructure.

The product offerings they have created are delivering fundamental value to businesses and consumers, and the market pull for that value will only grow. Trying to slow progress or demand is foolhardy; but leaving the economy to a handful of digital monopolies will be problematic for our companies, our staff, and our social systems. If we do not turn this tide—the increasing amount of wealth in the hands of tech giants, and the network effects of technologies making effective government regulation difficult at best—the consequences could be more dire than the mass company extinctions that we witnessed in the four previous ages.

We can create another future. We can make our organizations competitive. We can leverage the lessons of the tech giants and startups and adapt them to the complexity of our existing businesses. We can turn the black box of IT into a transparent network of value streams and manage those the way the digital natives of the Age of Software do. To achieve this, we need to shift our focus from transformation activities to measurable business results. We need a new framework to shift our organizations from project to product, thus securing our place in the digital future.

PART I

Flow Framework™

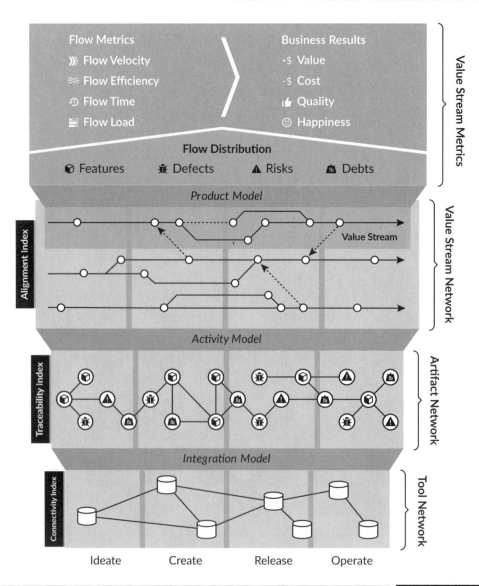

Flow Metrics
-))) Flow Velocity
- ✂ Flow Efficiency
- ⏱ Flow Time
- ☰ Flow Load

Business Results
- +$ Value
- -$ Cost
- 👍 Quality
- ☺ Happiness

Value Stream Metrics

Flow Distribution
- 🎁 Features
- 🐞 Defects
- ⚠ Risks
- 🛍 Debts

Product Model

Value Stream

Value Stream Network

Alignment Index

Activity Model

Artifact Network

Traceability Index

Integration Model

Tool Network

Connectivity Index

Ideate   Create   Release   Operate

PART I

THE FLOW FRAMEWORK

n the spring of 2017, Rene Te-Strote invited me to visit the BMW Group plant in Leipzig, Germany. My work with Rene started several years earlier, when we met at an industry conference on application life cycle management. Rene was the E/E-IT-Responsible for the electronic control units in the cars, and the BMW Group was looking for infrastructure tools to integrate and scale its software delivery toolchain. The tools were needed to support the increasing pace of software-component innovation demanded by the new i3 and i8 electric car programs.

Like others at the conference, Rene was looking to bring Agile and DevOps tools and methodologies into an enterprise IT environment. But what fascinated me was the scope of the problem that Rene was trying to solve. He not only needed to connect thousands of internal specialists—including developers, testers, and operations staff—he also needed to integrate dozens of software suppliers into that same toolchain. Each of the suppliers contributed to the over one hundred million lines of code that were run in a modern premium-class car.[1]

All that software, as well as the various internal software-delivery teams, had to be connected. For example, if the BMW Group's continuous integration environment identified a defect in a supplier's software, that defect needed to flow to the supplier's value stream, and then the fix needed to flow back to the BMW Group. Iterating on something as new as the i Series at the rate that the BMW Group was bringing them to market could not happen over transferring spreadsheets and reports.

Throughout our journey to solve this problem, I occasionally joked with Rene that if we succeeded, he ought to take me to the i Series plant and let me drive a car off the production line. As it turned out, Rene took me seriously.

Rene spent the first part of his career working in mass production at the Leipzig plant. The plant is one of the world's ultimate examples of how advanced mass production and manufacturing have become. The resulting visit to the BMW Group Leipzig plant turned out to be one of the most educational and inspirational experiences of my career. What I saw and learned in two full days of walking the plant floor and seeing the ground truth of the most advanced value streams from the Age of Mass Production gave me a new perspective on where we are in the maturity curve of the Age of Software.

In this book, I will walk you through the realizations I had on the factory floor, as they illustrate the errors of our approach to enterprise software delivery. I have, to the best of my memory, attempted to recreate the experience of visiting the Leipzig plant for you in the BMW stories that begin each chapter of this book.

Imagine Rene, who had been thrown from a world where a flawless car leaves the production line every seventy seconds to the world of enterprise IT that we know. The contrast could not have been starker, and I realized at that moment that this massive gap was what Rene wanted to show me. The gap went far beyond what we hear from Agile thought leaders who attempt to teach IT professionals Lean methods, such as those pioneered by the Toyota Production System (TPS). The gap demonstrated how disconnected enterprise IT organizations can be from the means of production. At the Leipzig plant, what amazed me most was the way that the business and manufacturing lines were seamlessly interconnected, all the way from the production lines to the business needs that were reflected in the architecture of the building complex itself.

Consider today's world of enterprise IT. Businesses measure IT with organizational charts and cost centers. The vast majority of enterprise IT organizations have no formalized notion of value streams or measurement of how business value is delivered. Perhaps most shockingly, they do not even agree on what the units of production are. Agile transformations keep failing to scale, with knee-jerk reactions of "culture" being to blame. Efforts that start out trying to deliver the end-to-end benefits of DevOps get pigeonholed into transformations that only involve "code commit to production"—such a narrow slice of the value stream that the business rarely sees the benefits or takes notice.

The bottom line is that enterprise IT organizations and the businesses in which they live have not yet caught up to the infrastructure and management techniques of the last technological revolution that have been mastered by companies like the BMW Group. Leadership clings to a Taylorist view, established in the Age of Steel, where IT organizations are siloed from the business, functionally specialized, and disconnected from each other. Yet those specialists are expected to deliver more and more as the threats of digital disruption grow. Many IT specialists know that this is a recipe for disaster, but the gap between technical language and business language has not been spanned. The result is that the software delivery efficiency of these companies is abysmal when compared to that of digital startups or the tech giants.

This mind-set has grave implications. If the current trajectory does not change, the incumbent companies that form the backbone of the world economy are at an inherent and significant disadvantage. Does this mean that large and established organizations in every industry are doomed to fail in an age where almost every enterprise is turning into a software company? A disconcerting trend is already visible across multiple markets. For example, at the start of the Age of Software, the average time in the Financial Times Stock Exchange was seventy-five years; today, it is less than twenty years and falling.[2]

The research and data summarized in this book offer a kernel of hope. Organizations can and must change in order to create the software innovation engines that will ensure their competitiveness and survival. To do that, we need to learn from the history of previous technological revolutions instead of assuming that we are in a completely unique moment in time. History may not repeat, but Perez's model suggests that it does have a rhythm.

The differences between manufacturing physical goods, which countless organizations mastered in the last age, and producing digital experiences are vast. The historical context differs as well. Attempts to blindly replicate what worked in the Age of Mass Production for the Age of Software can be catastrophically misleading, as we will see. We need a new way to think about and manage large-scale software delivery. This book proposes that new way.

The most important part of my trip to the Leipzig plant was an uneasy realization that blindly following in the footsteps of manufacturing is fraught with as much peril as not following them at all. Software production is vastly different—as the size of a software system grows, our ability to improve and manage it declines. Even so, we have learned to scale electrical distribution, car production, and other complex manufacturing processes, and we will learn to scale software production too. The problem is that, aside from a handful of exceptions, such as the tech giants, the vast majority of organizations have not yet learned how to effectively scale software delivery systems.

The market demands of large-scale software delivery present problems that most organizations are not equipped to handle. We need a new set of business concepts to understand software delivery at scale and a new kind of framework to manage it so that our businesses have the plasticity to evolve. Part I of this book examines the reach and the urgency of the problem and introduces the framework to overcome it.

In Part I, we will cover:

- *The reasons why your business will be affected by digital disruption, and how your thinking needs to change to survive the next ten years*

- *The three types of disruption and which one applies to your business*
- *An overview of the "Deployment Period" of the Age of Software and why understanding that matters for how you approach your digital transformation*
- *An introduction to the Flow Framework and the concept of software value streams*
- *An overview of the four flow items that define the delivery of business value*

CHAPTER 1

The Age of Software

Each technological revolution has resulted in the disruption of existing businesses by those who have mastered the new means of production. For example, in a matter of a few years, Uber demonstrated that a single, well-designed screen that is deployed at internet scale can disrupt an entire industry. An explosion of startups is threatening every aspect of every business as venture capital fuels the disruptions. In parallel, the tech giants continue to grow into new markets. Google and Facebook dominate nearly 90% of global spending on digital advertising,[1] while Amazon is on track to own a majority of the retail business and to use that leverage to expand into adjacent markets.[2] Every business leader needs to figure out when and how this affects them or risk their organization not surviving the next decade.

Each year, the stories and statistics look more dire. In 2017, the CEO of Equifax lost his job due to a security breach. Then, in a congressional hearing, he blamed the problem on a single software developer.[3] No CEO from a company that mastered the Age of Mass Production could blame such a cataclysmic business failure on something so seemingly trivial and manageable in their production system. (We will deconstruct the Equifax scenario further in Chapter 6.)

What's become clear is that no sector of the economy is safe, that the disruptions are accelerating, and that the very talented and highly trained business leaders responsible for the majority of the world's economy do not have the right set of tools and models to properly assess risk and capitalize on opportunity in the Age of Software.

The topic of *digital disruption* is not new and has been well documented. However, the significance of Carlota Perez's work is that disruption is a predictable outcome for companies that do not adapt to the new means of production. Companies that master the new means of production, even in slower moving parts of the market, will displace those that take more time to adapt. For example, an insurance company that provides a first-rate digital experience will displace the one that does not. And if the insurance sector itself does not move fast enough on the digital front, one of the tech giants could move into that market in search of a new vehicle for growth, turning displacement of specific companies into the disruption of an entire market. The examples in this chapter will highlight that no business is safe—no matter which industry sector or market it is in—because we are heading through the Turning Point of the Age of Software.

This book is not about business strategies for dealing with disruption. Books such as Geoffrey Moore's *Zone to Win: Organizing to Compete in an Age of Disruption* discuss how to adapt your business strategies to play disruption offense or defense. However, the problem is no longer that companies are unaware of their vulnerability to disruption. In 2017, for the first time, non-tech Fortune 500 companies made more investments in technology companies than technology companies did.[4] This is a sign that company leaders are starting to see the scope of the disruption and are using that to drive their digital transformations.

However, as we will learn in this chapter, the problem is that those transformations are failing. The main reasons for failure, according to *Altimeter*'s report "The 2017 State of Digital Transformation," are a shortage of digital talent and expertise (31.4%), general culture issues (31%), and the treatment of digital transformation as a cost center instead of an investment (31%).[5] None of these are root causes of transformation failure; rather, they are symptoms of a fundamental disconnect between business leaders and technologists that we will review throughout this book. This is not to say that talent is not critical; it is. But a project-oriented approach creates the conditions that push talent out of the organization instead of attracting talent to it.

The bottom line is that even with the best strategies and intentions, software delivery capacity and capabilities are a bottleneck in the digital transformation. Too little happens too slowly, and the business side does not understand why or what to do about it.

This chapter will start by reviewing how digital disruption is affecting the different sectors of the economy. It will address three types of disruption and discuss how software delivery capabilities are critical to navigating each. A summary of past technological revolutions will identify what we need to navigate this one. The chapter will conclude by introducing the "three epiphanies" that led to the Flow Framework—the mechanism for breaking the transformation failure cycle and ensuring that your company can survive the next ten years.

BMW TRIP Toward the Production Line

Entering the BMW Group Leipzig plant in Germany is an awe-inspiring experience. My hosts are Rene Te-Strote and Frank Schäfer. Frank is a plant manager responsible for overall vehicle integration. The enormous Central Building was designed by architect Zaha Hadid, who designed some of the most unique buildings of our time. The unapologetically sci-fi architecture invokes the feeling of walking into the future. The most prominent sight upon entering is an elevated and exposed section of the production line that towers high above eye level (Figure 1.1). Car bodies move across a suspended conveyor and then slowly disappear out of view as they glide over a sea of desks. The production line is visible to anyone who enters the building and to all the staff, and the entire building is designed around it. Every part of the building has some practical aspect related to manufacturing and value delivery. Everything embodies the maturity and scale of one of the masters of the Age of Mass Production.

Gene Kim, a mentor and coauthor of *The Phoenix Project: A Novel about IT, DevOps, and Helping Your Business Win* and *The DevOps Handbook*, once told me that we may only be 2% of the way there in the maturity of DevOps adoption.[6] This statement shocked me, but it also explained so much in terms of the glacial pace with which many traditional businesses move through the Age of Software. It's the slow rate of progress across the industry that is even more disconcerting than the 2% number itself. I became motivated to see firsthand what the culmination of the Age of Mass Production looked like so that I could extract every ounce of learning from it and apply those concepts to the Age of Software.

Figure 1.1: The BMW Group Leipzig Plant Central Building (with permission of the BMW Group)

A year prior to my visit to the Leipzig plant, the BMW Group celebrated its hundred-year anniversary with the "Next 100 Years" event, which recognized the past century of manufacturing excellence and presented the BMW Group's vision for the future of mobility. The event began with a quote from Alan Kay, of Xerox PARC fame, stating that "the best way to predict the future is to invent it."[7] What struck me most was just how different the next hundred years would be from the last.

The automotive industry is currently at an inflection point, where software-based innovation is starting to overtake the incremental gains in engine performance and other physical aspects of the car experience.

In 2017, the market cap of Tesla overtook Ford. Investors were betting big on the yet-unrealized potential for change embodied by Tesla, given that in 2016 Tesla produced 76 thousand cars versus Ford's 6.7 million and saw revenues of $7 billion versus Ford's $152 billion.[8]

In the Next 100 Years presentation, the BMW Group made it clear they were staying well ahead of the curve, building on their accomplishment of how quickly they brought the electric i3 and i8 cars to market. But that was not the most interesting part of the Next 100 Years vision, which projected a future of intelligent assistants, augmented and autonomous driving, and novel solutions to mobility that reframe the notion of car ownership.[9] The most interesting part of the Next 100 Years vision was that the innovations the BMW Group forecast were all powered by software, as underscored by an announcement from the BMW Group's CEO that said in the future the BMW Group expected more than half its staff to be software developers.[10]

I have witnessed similar inflection points at most of the Fortune 500 companies that I visit, regardless of the market segment they are in. Is every industry going to be disrupted in this way, where more than half the staff in years ahead are going to be IT professionals? Given Gene's "2% of the way there" comment, are all of these enterprise organizations prepared for that shift, from a company organization and management point of view? Did the BMW Group have some fundamental advantage, having mastered the last great technological revolution? What could we learn from the way this plant operated, and could we apply it to the way large-scale software is built?

No Sector Is Safe

Over the past two decades, the first companies exposed to the shift to digital communication and collaboration, such as Kodak and Blockbuster, were some of the first victims of disruption. The difference now is that the entire economy is exposed to disruption.

Consider the four economic sectors as laid out by Zoltan Kenessey. The primary sector involves resource extraction from the planet, the secondary involves processing and manufacturing, the tertiary involves services, and the quaternary involves knowledge work.[11]

The ability to improve discovery, extraction, and logistics through software gives some companies in the primary sector fundamental advantages over those who have not mastered these software-based solutions. While advances in extraction and technologies yield only incremental gains, software and IT systems can drive more transformational discoveries and efficiencies. For example, natural resource and energy companies are increasingly competing with software and data-driven approaches to discovery and extraction. The bottom line is that no business or sector is safe from digital disruption, even though the pace of the disruption will vary across sectors and businesses.

As we move out of the primary sector into the secondary, the shifts resulting from the Age of Software become more dramatic. Mass-manufactured goods, such as cars, have become commodities whose differentiation increasingly comes from a digital experience. Cars are now computers on wheels. Whereas your laptop's Microsoft Windows operating system may have sixty million lines of code,[12] in 2010 cars already contained around one hundred million.[13] For many automotive manufacturers, that makes the unit cost of the software in the car more expensive than the engine (Figure 1.2). This is only the start of the disruption. Autonomous drive systems will multiply the amount of software in the car and electrification of the engine is turning the rest of its core components into software systems as well.

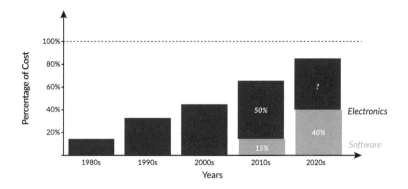

Figure 1.2: Software as Approximate Proportion of Car Cost

Bosch, one of the companies that embody the Age of Mass Production, announced in 2017 that it was hiring 20,000 specialists for its digital transformation, with nearly half of the jobs related to software.[14] Our physical products increasingly rely on a connected experience, and, as we'll learn in Chapter 7, factories, manufacturers, and assembly processes themselves are being transformed by software.

The digital disruptions and displacements we are witnessing in the tertiary sector (services) are spectacular. The software side of this story begins in 1997 with the transformation Netflix brought to the movie rental business. In those days, internet bandwidth was too scarce to deliver digital movies to the home. Inspired by computer scientist Andrew S. Tanenbaum's famous math problem, which asked students to figure out the bandwidth of a station wagon carrying tapes across the US, Reed Hastings (co-founder and CEO of Netflix) determined that software could be applied to the selection and logistical distribution of DVDs.[15] Not long after, venture capitalist Marc Andreessen described FedEx as "a software network that happens to have trucks, planes, and distribution hubs attached" in his seminal essay "Why Software is Eating the World."[16] What Netflix and FedEx realized is that software can yield exponential gains in logistics.

Even so, we are still at the early stages of disruption in retail and logistics. Amazon is now able to combine supply-chain data with both logistics and consumer spending habits, which could disrupt storefronts themselves. Just as Walmart disrupted other retailers by mastering the methods of the Age of Mass Production, Amazon is now doing the same to Walmart and other retailers by disrupting the supply chain and seeing a nearly identical market-share growth profile.[17] What's clear from these trends is that the companies that achieved even a small and early edge on applying software to consumer experiences and logistics have won a seemingly insurmountable edge over the rest of the industry.

Finally, the quaternary sector—composed of knowledge-work industries such as technology, media, education, and government—moves at an even faster rate of digital change by virtue of being the newest and most malleable sector, in terms of how software can affect distribution and infrastructure. For example, we have already seen multiple waves of collaboration technology within the Age of Software, ranging from email to instant messaging to teleconferencing and digital assistants. Whatever the sector, we now have enough data points from the disruptions to make the trend clear. It's happening in every sector, and the pace appears to be increasing. Companies that have harnessed software innovation are the winners, leaving those who fall behind to decline or get "Blockbustered."

Types of Disruption

While examples of disruptions abound, not all disruptions are equal. In order to understand how the impact of software delivery will affect your business, we need a model of the different kinds of digital disruptions. In *Zone to Win*, Geoffrey Moore provides a model that I will build on in this book. Moore's three types of disruption are the *Infrastructure Model*, *Operating Model*, and *Business Model* disruptions.[18] For most companies in the Age of Software, addressing disruptions will require mastering software delivery. However, the type of disruption that your business needs in order to play offense or defense will determine how you shape your IT investments and value streams.

Infrastructure Model disruptions are the easiest to address. They involve changes in how customers access a given product or offering; for example, requiring your products to be marketed via social media but not changing how you sell. The Infrastructure Model disruptions that we are seeing are competition-differentiated digital marketing and communication. Digital services are blending with the social networks that underpin the trust economy.

Operating Model disruptions rely on using software to change the relationship of the consumer with the business. For example, airlines must now provide a first-rate mobile phone experience or risk losing passenger bookings. The Operating Model here changes fundamentally, as agents and call centers play a diminishing role. Competing with startups on this front requires a first-rate digital experience. For example, a consumer bank can expect to be disrupted by new financial services startups that delight their users with better personal-finance management features.

Business Model disruptions involve a more fundamental application of software and technology to a business. This might mean a software and logistics innovation that cuts out a major manual step of consumers getting goods, such as a store visit. Moore states that established enterprises are not capable of disrupting themselves and, as such, must establish an innovation engine that will allow them to catch the next wave of disruption emerging in another market category.[19]

Whatever the examples are for your business, in order to win in the Age of Software you must precisely define which type or types of disruption put your business at risk. Wherever you land, the next step involves a significant investment in software delivery. The success of that initiative and your ability to win your market will be determined by your ability to define, connect, and manage your software value streams.

Unbundling of Every Industry

Consider your next car. Dozens of startups are competing to win a portion of your experience with automotive mobility. This ranges from connected car technology and autonomous driving to management of tire inflation and car repair. Each of these startups is competing with each other and with the incumbent automotive vendors who have traditionally owned all aspects of the car users experience. In Zone Management terms, these are only Infrastructure Model disruptions. Companies like Lyft, Uber, and Car2Go are in the midst of both Operating Model and Business Model disruptions by changing consumers' relationships with cars at the ownership level.

Shifting to finance, banks have been one of the leaders in technology adoption. Their business is fundamentally a knowledge-work business, and any technological advantage they can derive can quickly lead to a market advantage. For this reason, banks have been early adopters of new technologies; for example, many were running open-source software years before other enterprises had even considered using unsupported software produced by a collective of individuals who are not paid for their efforts. For the past decade, banks have been staffing ahead of digital disruption by hiring tens of thousands of

IT workers into their organizations. As an example of scale, Catherine Bessant, the head of Global Technology and Operations at Bank of America, has 95,000 employees and contractors reporting to her.[20]

There are hundreds of startups with venture funding who are targeting key aspects of a bank's business. Each offers a different product or service that exists because it stands to compete with those offered by the incumbents. Given the amount of financing we're seeing in finance technology, a report in 2016 found that over 1,000 fintech (finance technology) companies raised $105 billion in funding that's valued at $867 billion.[21]

A fundamental shift is happening. Even when staffed with tens of thousands of workers, the incumbents create and deliver software at a rate that appears to be leaving large and numerous doors open to disruption. And it's not for lack of discussion or investment to stay ahead of the startups or lack of finding creative ways to play offense or defense to the disruptors. Thanks to their ability to build and iterate on software quickly, and because they are unencumbered by existing customers or legacy systems, startups are innovating how customers interact with their products in services ranging from health insurance to cryptocurrencies.

The examples above illustrate how startups, financed by venture capital, are disrupting entrenched businesses and industries. The other vector of disruption is the tech giants that have mastered software production. Whatever the vector of disruption, before setting a plan of action we must examine where we sit in this technological revolution and what the upcoming wave of change and disruption will look like.

We Are Entering the Deployment Period

Will this pace of disruption continue indefinitely at its current pace? Will the amount of venture capital fueling the growth of startups continue to rise to the point where it is futile for entrenched companies to compete? Will the majority of the economy soon be owned by the tech giants?

Answers to these questions are consequential for our organizations, as they can help guide what and how we invest in our digital strategies in order to survive the Turning Point, the period between the Installation and Deployment Periods that is marked by a financial crash and recovery. Without understanding these questions, our efforts could be as misguided as investing in teams of horses to compete in the Age of Steam & Railways. And as we will see in the next chapter, that is precisely what the majority of enterprise IT organizations are doing.

Several theories exist to explain technological innovation cycles and their impact on the economy. Kondratiev waves (described as fifty-year cycles of expansion, stagnation, and recession that result from technological innovation and entrepreneurship) and cycles of *Creative Destruction* (the process of industrial mutation that incessantly revolutionizes the economic structure from within, destroying the old one and incessantly creating a new one) are concepts introduced by Joseph Schumpeter in the 1930s in his book *Capitalism, Socialism, and Democracy*.[22] The economist Carlota Perez has expanded on these concepts in her profound book *Technological Revolutions and Financial Capital*.[23]

There is disagreement among economists as to the Kondratiev waves' cause and duration. For example, while some predict that the current wave will be longer, others propose that the waves have been shortening consecutively.[24]

Though the exact length of the current wave cannot yet be determined, Perez's work provides us with a model for distinguishing between the technological systems of the last age from this one, and for using that to better understand how to master the means of production in the Age of Software. (A summary of Perez's work is available in the blog post "The Deployment Age" by Jerry Neumann, a prominent venture capitalist.)[25]

For the purpose of understanding where we are within the Age of Software, the most important aspect of Perez's theory is the concept of the Installation Period and the Deployment Period of new technological systems (Figure 1.3). In the Installation Period, large amounts of financial capital, such as venture capital, are deployed to leverage the new technological system that has formed a critical mass of technology, companies, and access to capital in order to disrupt the age that came before it. This is exactly what we have been witnessing with the Cambrian explosion of startups.

Following the Installation Period is a Deployment Period, where companies that master the means of production earn increasingly larger portions of the economy and the new infrastructure. This creates a period where *production capital*, a good portion of it controlled by the new technology giants of that age, starts displacing startups and financial capital. Production capital is different from financial capital in that it is controlled by company managers who are seeking innovations to make production more efficient by working within established companies (versus the radical and risky innovations with high multiples favored by financial capital). During the Deployment Period, financial capital and startups begin looking for a new home by placing bets on what the next technological revolution could be.

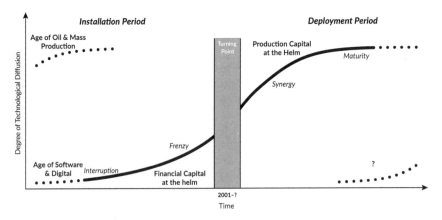

Figure 1.3: From Installation Period to Deployment Period[26]

This pattern has repeated itself four times over, as is visible in Table 1.1. In her book, Perez provides evidence that we are in the midst of the fifth iteration.[27] The Age of Software began around 1970, with the introduction of the microprocessor. In 2002, Perez predicted that around the Turning Point, the point between the Installation Period and Deployment Period, the new masters of production would amass enough wealth and control that governments would start imposing regulations, and we are seeing evidence of that today.[28]

We cannot conclusively determine where exactly we are with respect to the Turning Point or how long it will last. We do not know whether age will be materially different from others. In an interview, Perez told me that this particular Turning Point appears to keep drawing itself out longer and longer.[29] However, by the time we know the precise shape of this age, it will be too late to do anything about it, as those who were early to mastering the new means of production will have displaced those who were too late.

Installation-Deployment	Age	New Technological Systems	New Infrastructure	Triggering Innovations	Managerial Innovations
1771–1829	Industrial Revolution	Water-powered mechanization	Canals, turnpike roads, sailing ships	Arkwright's Cromford Mill (1771)	Factory Systems, entrepreneurship, partnerships
1829–1873	Age of Steam & Railways	Steam-powered mechanization and transport	Railways, telegraph, steam ships	Liverpool-Manchester Railway (1831)	Joint stock companies, subcontracting
1875–1918	Age of Steel and Heavy Engineering	Electrification of equipment and transport	Steel railways, steel ships, global telegraph	Carnegie's steel plant (1875)	Professional management systems, giant firms Taylorism
1908–1974	Age of Oil & Mass Production	Motorization of transport and economy	Radio, motorways, airports	Ford's Highland Park assembly line (1913)	Mass production and consumption, Fordism, Lean
1971–?	Age of Software & Digital	Digitization of the economy	Internet, software, cloud computing	Intel microprocessor (1971)	Networks, platforms, venture capital

Table 1.1: Technological Revolutions[30]

From today's vantage point, we see ongoing examples of financial capital at play, such as the stories of the "unbundlings" of various industries caused by the number of new startups funded by venture capital. However, we are also starting to see the effects of production capital as well.

Consider Jawbone, a nimble digital native funded by top-tier venture capitalists with no lack of access to capital. Jawbone created multiple category-defining products, ranging from Bluetooth headsets to wireless speakers to wearable fitness trackers. In total, Jawbone raised $930 million of financial capital between 2006 and 2016 from top-tier firms, but ultimately it ended up in an asset sale, making it the second-costliest venture-capital-backed startup of all time.[31]

Even with the combination of innovation and great products, Jawbone lost out to production-capital companies like Apple. The smartwatch innovator Pebble closed its doors in December 2016 for similar reasons.[32] In addition to this growing graveyard of consumer hardware startups, it is becoming increasingly difficult to launch a new social media company that gets to scale before Facebook either acquires or destroys it.[33] These growing effects of production capital are signals of our passing through the Turning Point.

While we do not know how long this Turning Point will last, if it follows Perez's model of a five-decade cycle and we know we have been seeing the signs of the Installation Period since the 1970s, then we can assume that with each year we are getting closer to the Deployment Period. Once we reach the Deployment Period, companies that have not adapted to the new means of production will decline in relevance and market share. In the next decade, a significant number will lose their place in the market. We have seen other companies try and fail to scale their IT, then Agile, and now DevOps transformations in a meaningful time frame. For many of these companies, this is the last call if they want to have a fighting chance at surviving the latest technological age, let alone the next.

Three Epiphanies

My career has been dedicated to understanding and improving how large-scale software is built. I spent nearly two decades working on new programming languages and software development tools, and have had a chance to work with some of the best technologists in the world. But I have come to realize that, due to where we are in the Turning Point, technology improvements are no longer the bottleneck.

Technology improvements will be relevant but incremental, yielding productivity gains of less than ten percent to organizations via new programming languages, tools, frameworks, and runtimes.

In contrast, the disconnect between the business and IT is massive, as are the disconnects within IT organizations. The common approach to enterprise architecture is wrong, as it tends to focus on the needs of the technologists and not on the flow of business value. Contrast this with the BMW Group's Leipzig plant, where the entire plant is designed around the changing needs of the business, from the extensibility of the buildings to the modularity of the production lines themselves.

For me, the realization that technologists' pursuits were bringing diminishing returns did not come as a single eureka moment. Rather, I had separate realizations, each of which caused me to make a major pivot in my career. Each of these "epiphanies" involved a collection of experiences that reframed my view of software delivery and kept me awake through the night as I slowly digested how many of my previous assumptions were flawed.

The first epiphany came from my first job as a developer working on a new programming language. During that time, I realized the problem we were solving spanned well beyond the source code. The second epiphany came from a culmination of hundreds of meetings with enterprise IT leaders that made it clear to me that the approach to managing software delivery and transformations was fundamentally broken. The third epiphany came during my visit to the BMW plant and revealed that the entire model that we have for scaling software delivery is wrong. (I will expand on these epiphanies in Part III.) Each epiphany is connected by our trying—and failing—to apply concepts from previous technological revolutions to this one. To summarize, my three epiphanies were:

- **Epiphany 1:** Productivity declines and waste increases as software scales due to disconnects between the architecture and the value stream.
- **Epiphany 2:** Disconnected software value streams are the bottleneck to software productivity at scale. These value stream disconnects are caused by the misapplication of the project management model.

- **Epiphany 3:** Software value streams are not linear manufacturing processes but complex collaboration networks that need to be aligned to products.

The first epiphany—that software productivity declines and waste increases when developers are disconnected from the value stream—came as the result of a personal crisis. While on the research staff at Xerox PARC, I was an open-source software developer and consistently worked seventy to eighty hours per week. Most of that time was spent coding, plus regularly sleeping under my office desk to complete the cliché. The number of hours at the mouse and keyboard resulted in a seemingly insurmountable case of repetitive strain injury (RSI). It grew progressively worse, along with the heroics and coding required to get release after release out, and my boss repeatedly cautioned me that he'd seen several PARC careers end in this way. With the staff nurse offering little help beyond advising caution and providing ibuprofen, I realized that every single mouse click counted.

This led me to do PhD research by joining Gail Murphy and the Software Practices Lab that she created at the University of British Columbia. As mouse clicks became my limiting factor, I started tracking the events for each click by instrumenting my operating system, and I came to realize that the majority of my RSI-causing activity was not producing value; it was just clicking between windows and applications to find and refind the information I needed to get work done.

I then expanded my research to six professional developers working at IBM, and I extended the monitoring and added an experimental developer interface for aligning coding activity around the value stream. The results were surprising to both Gail and I, so we decided to extend the study to "the wild" by recruiting ninety-nine professional developers working within their organizations and having them send before-and-after traces of all of their development activity. (The full findings are detailed in Chapter 7 and were published at the International Symposium on Foundations of Software Engineering.)[34]

The conclusion was clear: as the size of our software systems grew, so did the distance between the architecture and the effort it took to add one of the hundreds of features being requested by our end users.

The number of collaboration and tracking systems we used grew as well, causing yet more waste and duplicate entry. These findings were the inspiration for Gail and I to found Tasktop, a software company dedicated to better understanding this problem.

Several years later, while getting an overview of a large financial institution's toolchain, I had the second epiphany. This problem of thrashing was not unique to developers; it was a key source of waste for any professional involved in software delivery, from business analysts to designers, testers, and operations and support staff. The more software delivery specialists involved, the more disconnects formed between them and the more time was spent on thrashing, duplicate data entry, or the endless status updates and reports.

The challenges I was personally facing from my declining productivity and increased thrashing were being mirrored, at scale, across thousands of IT staff. The more staff, the more tools, and the more software scale and complexity, the worse this problem became. For example, after conducting an internal study on one bank's software delivery practices, we determined that, on average, every developer and test practitioner was wasting a minimum of twenty minutes per day on duplicate data entry between two different Agile and issue-tracking tools. In some cases, that grew to two hours per day, and the overhead for first-line managers was even higher. When we dug deeper into how developers spent their time, we found that only 34% of a developer's active working time at the keyboard went to reading and writing code.[35] Yet this is what developers are paid to do and what they love to do. This was a deep and systemic problem.

As Gail and I started working more with enterprise IT organizations, we realized just how different this world was from the much simpler and more developer-centric world of open source, startups, and tech companies, but we lacked empirical data on enterprise IT delivery. At the BMW Group plant, I was simply able to look down at the line to see the flow of work. Unfortunately, no data was available on how work flows across the tools that form a value stream across enterprise IT organizations. But we now had a broad enterprise IT customer base, including close to half of the Fortune 100, and realized that we had a very unique data set, as the majority of those organizations had shared with us all the tools involved in their value stream and the artifacts that flow across those tools. We collected and analyzed 308 Agile, Application Lifecycle Management (ALM), and DevOps toolchains from these organizations. We started calling these *tool networks* once we saw how the tools were interconnected. (See Chapter 8 for more.) In the process, I personally met with the IT leaders of over two hundred of those organizations to better understand what we were seeing in the data.

With those 308 value stream diagrams in mind, while walking over ten kilometers (about six miles) of the Leipzig plant production line, I felt the kernel of the third epiphany form. The entire model for how we think about a software value stream is wrong. It is not a pipeline or a linear manufacturing process that resembles an automotive production line; it is a complex collaboration network that needs to be connected and aligned to the internal and external products created by an IT organization, and to business objectives.

This is what the data was telling us, yet this approach is completely at odds with the project- and cost-oriented mentality with which enterprise organizations are managing IT investment. The ground truth (that is, the truth learned through direct observation) of these enterprise tool networks is telling us that all the specialists in IT are already starting to work in this new way by adopting Agile teams and DevOps automation, but these specialists lack the infrastructure and business buy-in to do so effectively.

On the flip side, the business is further losing the ability to see or manage the work that the technologists are doing. Leadership seems to be using managerial tools and frameworks from one or two technological ages ago, while the technologists are feeling the pressure to produce software at a rate and feedback cycle that can never be met with these antiquated approaches. The gap between the business and technologists is widening through transformation initiatives that were supposed to narrow it. We need to find a better way.

Conclusion

An amazing effect of the BMW Group Leipzig plant is that it places visitors and employees at the juxtaposition of the last phase of the

Deployment Period of the Age of Mass Production and the Installation Period of the Age of Software. You can watch the culmination of advanced manufacturing and factory automation producing cars that are increasingly powered by software. In contrast, the world's top enterprise IT organizations are more like the nearly three hundred car manufacturers that were trying to master production in Detroit in the 1900s but went extinct while the likes of Ford pulled ahead.[36]

In this chapter, we saw the scale of the change that is happening due to the maturation of the Age of Software. The biggest problem is that, at a managerial level, established businesses are using the managerial and production methods of previous ages, and thus, are failing in this one. In the next chapter, we will dive into the evidence collected from enterprise IT organizations that shows the symptoms of this problem, and we'll highlight the cause of organizations' failure to transform. After that, we'll explore the solution.

CHAPTER 2

From Project to Product

Transformation may be the most overused term in IT. However, when looked at through the historical lens of technological revolutions, the overuse is less surprising, as it is rooted in an existential problem for companies faced with the need to embrace change in order to survive the Turning Point.

In this age, survival is dependent on an organization's ability to deliver software products and digital experience. Underscoring the scale and urgency, IDC, a market research firm, has estimated digital transformation as an $18.5 trillion opportunity by 2020, which represents 25% of the global GDP.[1] Those that succeed will reap the rewards and displace those that do not. Many large organizations have already kicked off their transformation initiatives; others are noticing their software investment creeping up on them, with CFOs often the first to realize how much of next year's budget and headcount is related to IT.

In the Age of Mass Production, IT was a separate silo that played a supporting function, enabling the productivity of other means of production, such as facilitating communication or sales force automation. IT will continue to play a key supporting function in that regard; for example, the kinds of factory automation envisioned by Industry 4.0 will yield significant productivity results in mass production through the "cyber physical systems" proposed in Industry 4.0 initiatives.[2] However, these are extensions of the last Installation Period, and they are less disruptive than the change in markets and business models that are now happening. But in the Age of Software, digital technology has become the core of the organization and cannot be compartmentalized to an isolated department.

So, how do our organizations and managerial techniques need to adapt? In this chapter, we will examine two transformations that failed even though they were formed with the best of intentions for surviving the Age of Software. The first was an Agile transformation failure that contributed to Nokia losing the mobile market. The second involves a large financial institution we'll call LargeBank that spent $1 billion on an Agile and DevOps transformation without delivering any measurable increase in the delivery of business value. Both of these failures share a common thread of how paradigms that worked in previous ages can fail us in this one.

Next, we'll discuss the project management paradigm and why it creates a chasm between the business and IT. We'll look at the creation of the Boeing 787 Dreamliner and contemplate how it exemplifies product thinking. Then we'll review why moving from project-oriented management to product-oriented management is critical for connecting software delivery to the business, and how shifting our managerial perspective from project to product paves the path for success in the Age of Software.

Before we dive into the Flow Framework and its inception, it's important to look at how operations at the BMW Group Leipzig plant illustrate the success of a different way of measuring flow and of defining software value streams along product lines.

BMW TRIP Discovering the Plant Architecture

The Central Building opens into an enormous open space. To the left is the exposed production line, with car bodies moving steadily past as large, orange robotic arms swivel and dip to put the cars together piece by piece. Combined with the futuristic architecture, the entire space has the feeling of entering a building where the next version of the starship *Enterprise* could be manufactured.

"Is it possible that a certain kind of architecture can positively influence teamwork and productivity within a plant?" the plant brochure asks. "The Central Building of the BMW Group

Leipzig plant, designed by the famous architect Zaha Hadid, is the implementation of this idea. This unique building is the center of communication, and it connects all production areas."

All of IT sits to the right of the exposed production line.

"The plant CIO's desk is right over there." Rene points to a sea of several hundred desks and dual-monitor workstations to the right of the exposed production line.

It hadn't occurred to me that the plant would have its own CIO with a sizeable IT infrastructure and staff, but given the scale of operations that is visible, there must be countless internal applications managing everything from supply chains to final assembly.

Each of the people is wearing a blue vest, blue jacket, or entirely blue jumpsuit. Some of the blue apparel hangs on chairs and desks. Rene hands me a vest with my name embroidered on it, which gives me the feeling of belonging in the building the moment I put it on.

"These vests are antistatic," Frank says. "You must wear them at all times around the production line. We will also attach special static dischargers to your shoes." He hands me discharge stickers from his vest pocket.

"All plant staff wear these, including the IT staff, the CIO, and the CEO," says Rene.

Most of the startups I have visited have branded clothing to communicate their identity and culture, with T-shirts and hoodies being the most common. But there is something more to the form and function of these vests.

We watch the 1- and 2-Series cars moving along the production line. Rene explains, "In 2017, we produced 980 cars each day, with a new car being completed every seventy seconds. Everything that you are about to see ensures we can achieve these production rates and flow. Later in the day, we will also see one of the newest innovations of the plant, the production of the i3 and i8."

I recall from the brochure that the plant was a two-billion-euro investment representing the "peak of production, automation, and sustainability."[3] That cost is in the ballpark of a semiconductor fabrication plant. But whereas modern chip "fabs" are built around creating the same cutting-edge processor over and over, something different is happening here.

Each vehicle is made specifically to a customer's order. This exemplifies the idea of "just in time." Just-in-time approaches delay processing and other work until the last moment the work can be done economically, thus optimizing workflow and resource use.

"Not only does the plant implement just-in-time inventory," Rene continues, "the cars are manufactured just-in-sequence."

"The cars come off the production line in the same sequence that customer orders are placed. Each car is tailor-made to the customer's specifications and preferences," Frank adds.

"The cars remain in the same order on their entire journey on the production line?" I am having trouble grasping how they could implement this.

"Interesting question," Frank continues. "No, there is one part of the production line where the car bodies need to be taken out of sequence. Then they need to be temporarily inventoried, and after that, put back into sequence. It is a very complex process and is the bottleneck of our plant."

"So, where is the bottleneck?" I ask, in what must have registered with Frank as a combination of overeagerness and naiveté.

"This entire building is designed around the bottleneck. But before we look at that, let's go to the Assembly Building," Frank says.

As Frank leads us along the exposed production line, I take out my phone and open up maps in satellite mode. I see dozens of large and interconnected buildings (Figure 2.1). The arrangement of buildings looks strikingly similar to the computer motherboards that I used back in the days when I would assemble my own PCs—so much so that I do a double take and stop walking for a moment. The Central Building looks like a CPU and its interconnects.

"Ah, yes, there we are," Frank says as he uses the satellite map to explain the plant's layout. "Here you see the Central Building, and you can see that we are nearing the Assembly Building. The structure of the Assembly Building is very interesting," Frank continues. "We call this the 'five fingers' structure."

The massive building did indeed have the shape of rectangular fingers and a hand.

1. Central Building
2. Body shop
3. Paint shop
4. Assembly
5. Supply centers

Figure 2.1: The BMW Group Leipzig Plant
(with permission of the BMW Group)

"In software architecture, you have extensibility," says Rene. "Maybe it is hard to see, but this plant is also architected for extensibility along its main production lines."

"Yes," adds Frank. "When additional production steps are added to the line, we are able to extend the length of the 'fingers.' The buildings have been extended over time as we have expanded and added more automation and more production steps. You see that the 'fingers' are different lengths."

Frank then points at a building that stands out from the rest. It is white in color but also attached to the "hand."

"The 'hand' houses the 1- and 2-Series production lines," Frank says. "That building is a newer one. It is where we make the i3 and i8 electric cars."

I want to get a better look at this building and instinctively clicked the "3-D" button on the map. It goes into a "flyover" mode and starts navigating around the building.

"Look there," says Frank. "You see those trucks?"

He points at large trucks that are connected right to the "fingers" of the assembly building.

"As Rene mentioned earlier, the plant functions with just-in-time inventory. Any stockpiled inventory would be waste. So, the parts are delivered 'just in time,' right to the part of the assembly line where they are used. The BMW Group has around 12,000 suppliers worldwide, so this is quite an operation," says Frank. "Let's skip the bottleneck for now, as we have to go to that area at lunch anyway. Let me take you right to the 1- and 2-Series production line."

We walk into the Assembly Building and onto a catwalk suspended three stories in the air and looking along the length of the "hand." It is an extraordinarily vast space, and processing the scale takes a few moments. The scene is so visually complex that it is difficult to grasp. But this complexity is nothing like the chaos and clamor of Times Square on a busy summer day. Instead, perfect order and coordination of hundreds of machines and moving parts were orchestrated at what seemed a mind-boggling scale.

This massive mechanical ballet produces some of the most complex objects made by humanity. Over 12,000 suppliers, over 30,000 parts in each car, and immense functional specialization along the line, producing a new car every seventy seconds in the sequence that customer orders are made.

"By the way, Mik, you cannot take out your phone again," Frank says in a friendly but unmistakably serious way.

Agile Transformation Failure at Nokia

The idea of drawing on automotive manufacturing lessons and applying them to software is not new. Countless books on Agile methods draw on Lean manufacturing and the Toyota Production System in particular. While I was already familiar with that literature when I visited the BMW Group plant, the difference between what I thought I understood about advanced manufacturing and what I learned at the plant was enormous.

My journey using Agile methods for day-to-day software delivery started in 1999, in the relatively small scale of a single team working on an open-source project and using Kent Beck's Extreme Programming (XP) methodology. Ten years later, at the Agile 2009 conference, I presented what I learned from adapting Agile methods to an open-source project that I was leading. It was my first time at the conference, and the most interesting thread I noticed was that of scaling Agile.

Numerous consultants were using Nokia as proof that Agile development methodologies scaled to large enterprises. The "Nokia Test" was cited frequently.[4] It was a simple method of determining whether an organization was following Scrum. The test was developed by Nokia Siemens Networks, and it further cemented Nokia as the namesake and poster child of scaling Agile.

I saw the potential for scaling Agile and was thrilled when my company got the opportunity to start working with Symbian, the mobile operating system (OS) Nokia had acquired in 2008. My first meeting with a CIO was with Symbian's, later in 2009. That led to Nokia becoming Tasktop's first enterprise customer, when we supported a project on connecting Agile tools to developer workflow. Nokia and Symbian had some tremendous visionaries internally, in addition to hiring the best external contractors and thought leaders to help guide their transformation.

The problem was that the entire effort was set up for failure in spite of the leadership's best intentions and the organization's willingness to transform. A lot of energy fueled the transformation. Everyone was saying and appeared to be doing the right things, and the various consultants and vendors were indicating that they were on track.

The "Nokia Test" offered a series of questions on whether development was done iteratively and whether it followed the principles of Scrum, allowing a mechanism for testing each team to determine the state of how Agile they were. I was genuinely impressed by the sheer scale of Nokia's commitment to their Agile transformation and the degree to which the company and the teams that we worked with tracked activities to the impressive Agile model that they had created. It was clear that the executives had realized how much Agile could benefit the company in terms of their ability to adapt to the rapidly changing market.

However, as I worked with more development teams, the writing on the wall became evident. What struck me was the degree to which the activities and adherence to the model were being measured without a clear sense of the outcomes surfacing through those activities. Given that we were providing open-source tools to Nokia's developers, we started interacting more and more with the developers and noticed this disconnect became even more prominent as we worked our way toward the leaves of the organizational chart—the development teams.

In order to figure out how we could better connect the delivery layer and the planning layer, I realized it was time to get a sense of the ground truth. I asked my main contact whether I could interview some engineers across various teams to get a better sense of what was going on. The results were eye opening.

The developers I spoke to had no issue with any of the Agile practices and were mildly favorable of them; they had much bigger problems. They had major issues downstream from them because of the long build/test/deploy loop that was partly due to Nokia's otherwise formidable software security processes. They had even more significant issues with the architecture of the Symbian OS, which was making many of the changes the business wanted to bring to market difficult or overly time consuming to implement. The Symbian OS was not structured for the kind of extensibility that was needed; for example, it could not support the installation of third-party applications or what we now call an "app store."

Finally, while the developers were positive on Scrum overall, their daily work was disconnected from the higher-level planning that was being done with a whole different set of tools. The enterprise-level Agile tool that was selected was not being used by the developers, who preferred simpler developer-centric tools. Instead, they would document the work completed for the release at the end of the iteration (or "sprint"), after the work was done, as user stories (a description of a software feature from an end-user perspective). The tool, which had all the features of a modern best-of-breed Agile tool, effectively became a documentation tool, not the mechanism for flow and feedback that had been intended.

After conducting those interviews, I realized that the transformation was in trouble. In hindsight, this was nothing like what I saw at the Leipzig plant, where every production metric relevant to the business was understood, well defined, visible, and automated. In addition, at the plant, the business side intimately understood car production. In contrast, at Nokia, the tie-in between business outcomes and software production metrics was either not explicit or nonexistent.

In every way that it was being measured, the transformation was on track—all of the right activities were happening, right down to the adoption of the Agile tool. But the developers were suffering from major friction, both in what it took to build code and in what it took to deploy it. Even more consequential was how difficult adding features had become due to the size and architecture of the Symbian OS.

If the transformation had been measured according to outcomes or results instead of activities, the picture would have looked much different. The fundamental bottlenecks that the developers were encountering would have surfaced. The investment needed in Nokia's core platform, the Symbian OS, could have been made in a way that would allow it to compete with new, software-savvy entrants to the market, like Apple. But that crucial feedback was not making it back to the business because of the way development was disconnected from the business. And the downstream disconnects and inefficiencies in building and deploying the software meant that any progress in improving this would run at too slow a pace.

At a business level and as a market leader, Nokia was well aware that it needed to move and adjust quickly in the rapidly evolving mobile ecosystem. This was the reason to roll out Agile in the first place: to more quickly adapt to that marketplace and the growing role of software within it. Though the proxy metrics could deem the Nokia Agile transformation a success, the lack of actual business results of that transformation contributed to the business' failure and inability to shift from elegant handsets and buttons to a software and screen-centric mobile experience.

This is not to say that Nokia made no strategic missteps on the hardware front. For example, Nokia was slow to move to the capacitive touchscreens that Apple innovated with the launch of the iPhone.[5] But Nokia's strengths were on the hardware front; and in the end, they lost to two vendors with hardened software expertise when Apple's iOS and Google's Android OS took over as the mobile platforms of choice.

Nokia had an engine and infrastructure for innovating on the hardware front that was a pinnacle of the Age of Mass Production, but they did not have an effective engine and infrastructure for the Age of Software and did not have the management metrics or practices in place to realize that until it was too late.

If we step back and imagine Nokia's end-to-end value stream, the Agile transformation was a local optimization of the value stream. In other words, while a tremendous amount of investment went into the transformation, the bottleneck to delivering an operating system capable of supporting a mobile ecosystem was not the Agile teams.

Was it downstream of the Agile teams, in a lack of continuous integration and delivery capability? Was it in the architecture itself, which could not support the kinds of feature and product delivery that were needed? Or was it upstream of development and closer to the business, which was so disconnected from delivery and the architectural investment needed, such as technical debt reduction, that they did not realize Agile planning would fail to drive any of the desired results?

My interviews hinted at these issues, and I got the sense that there was no business-level understanding of what the real bottleneck was, as the gulf between what IT and developers knew and what the business assumed was so vast. That, in turn, led to the Agile transformation—implemented as a local optimization of the end-to-end value stream—yielding little result and not addressing the bottleneck.

Even if the teams had attained a theoretical ideal of agility, would Nokia have been able to adapt more quickly without upstream changes to how the business was measuring delivery? Or adapt downstream changes in how the software was deployed? Or the architecture changes that were slowing developers down in the first place?

In my opinion, that narrow-minded and activity-oriented view of Agile was the root cause of Nokia's failed digital transformation. The failed transformation made fast iteration and learning from the market impossible, as the lead times for delivering new features, such as an app store and an elegant home screen, were far too slow. This hindered the business's ability to learn and adapt, and that inability to adapt was a key factor in Nokia's downfall.

Lesson One: *To avoid the pitfalls of local optimization, focus on the end-to-end value stream.*

In the context of a software value stream, the concept of "end-to-end" includes the entire process of value delivery to the customer. It encompasses functions ranging from business strategy and ideation all the way to instrumentation of usage to determine which values were most adopted by the customer base. It is this end-to-end process that we need to understand and find bottlenecks in before considering the optimization of any particular segment of the process, such as feature design or deployment.

Contrast the approach that Nokia took with the BMW Group story earlier in this chapter. The entire Leipzig plant is designed to make the value stream visible, and the buildings are architected around the bottleneck. The architecture of the buildings is extensible to support the evolution of production technologies and changes in market conditions. Nokia had this level of maturity for its devices, but in spite of mastering mass production, it was not able to make the pivot into applying these lessons to software delivery.

Next, we will further analyze the reasons why this disconnect between the business and IT created an environment in which the business was set up for failure in its efforts to undergo a digital transformation.

DevOps to the Rescue?

It is tempting to blame the failure of Nokia's software transformation on Agile or Scrum. But this argument is just as flawed as claiming that Nokia was a success case for Scrum in 2009. Nokia's problems were not with Agile or Scrum; many organizations have had significant success adopting the exact methods that Nokia adopted with Scrum. No matter how effective Agile or Scrum could have been for Nokia, the organization's problems lay beyond the boundaries of Agile development teams.

Eliyahu M. Goldratt's theory of constraints and its applicability to Agile software development are discussed in Kent Beck's book *Extreme Programming Explained*.[6] Goldratt famously explained how investments made in areas other than the bottleneck are futile.[7] This was the futility of Nokia's Agile transformation. Nokia could have had the most supportive leadership and culture on the planet, transformed twice as fast, achieved twice the agility, and invested twice as much into the Agile transformation and still have seen no change in the slope of their decline due to the fact that the effort was not being applied at the bottleneck. What's worse, the outcomes of the effort were not being measured.

Could adoption of DevOps practices such as continuous delivery have turned the tide at Nokia? Possibly. Some of these practices were already in place, like automated testing. In my interviews, the subjects reported major inefficiencies that would have been addressed by the other key practices summarized in *The DevOps Handbook*—the automation of the entire deployment pipeline and support for small batch sizes.[8] In my experience, those practices are critical to an effective value stream, and if they are not adopted, it is only a matter of time before they become the bottleneck.

However, it would be incorrect to assume that applying DevOps practices to their delivery pipeline would have altered the curve of Nokia's decline. For example, if there was a managerial or cultural misalignment between the business and development, that could have been the bottleneck, and there were signs of that. Or if the architecture was as tangled as some of the engineers were concerned it was, that could have been the bottleneck. In hindsight, the most shocking aspect of this was that nobody could see the whole value stream, so nobody knew. Yet massive bets and investments on the transformation were being placed at the leadership level.

Had Nokia adopted the Three Ways of DevOps (Figure 2.2), they would have at least started on the path to identifying the bottleneck. By focusing on "flow" and "feedback" from Dev to Ops, Nokia might have seen indications of very long lead times for deployment. And "continual learning," if elevated beyond just development leaders, might have caused company leadership to start asking the right questions about organizational structure or the software architecture.

Or not. Nokia could have taken a very tactical approach to DevOps transformation, focused on continuous integration and application release automation alone, and not noticed the architectural or organizational bottlenecks. At a managerial level, they were missing the infrastructure and visibility that would allow them to see what was going on in their value stream. If treated like they treated Agile, DevOps would have been relegated to a technical practice rather than being elevated to the business, and would not have altered the outcome.

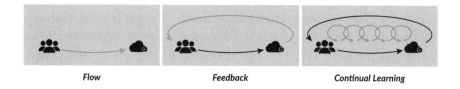

Flow	Feedback	Continual Learning

Figure 2.2 : The Three Ways of DevOps

Failing to Transform: The Story of LargeBank

The Nokia failure happened at a time when both scaled Agile and DevOps practices were less broadly understood. The story of this next transformation started with similarly noble goals but also resulted in a failure to deliver business results, even though it happened much more recently. This story, as well as the need to better understand why these failures happen instead of giving up on the organizations that seem to be struggling with the transition, drove me to study why the principles of DevOps and Agile appear to break down at scale.

I vividly recall sitting on a Boeing Dreamliner in June 2016 en route from Europe to my home and office in Vancouver, Canada, and reflecting on a particular meeting I had had with IT leadership at a bank. I was seated near the wings and admiring their organic-looking beauty; their flexible carbon-composite materials allowed them to swoop upward, reducing drag. This was long before my visit to the BMW Group plant, but it is the first recollection I have of a profound mental struggle to understand how, across the industry, we can be so good at making airplanes and cars while only a small portion of companies have truly mastered making software at scale. After staring at the wing's subtle shifts for an hour, I realized that my mind was stuck, as if on a Zen koan that I could not unfold.

This bank, which we'll refer to as LargeBank and of which I have redacted all identifying details, was undergoing the most massive IT transformation I had ever encountered. LargeBank is one of the top twenty-five financial institutions on the planet, and the project itself was an incredibly impressive set of Gantt charts that fit together like puzzle pieces along a precisely defined two-year time frame and touched on all parts of a multi-billion-dollar IT organization. Notably, this same story has unfolded in similar ways at other large institutions.

It was my third visit to LargeBank, and I had gone approximately every two years. Each time, the discussions were part of a large digital transformation initiative that the bank was undertaking, and this was attempt number three in a process that never changed. Many tool vendors, consultants, and other experts would be brought in. Since my company's business involves integrating various Agile and DevOps tools, we would be walked in detail through every tool and process that was involved in the transformation. Then, two years down the road, we would hear that the transformation had failed to deliver results, and the VP or SVP responsible would be fired. When the next transformation started, I would meet some of the new leadership and listen to the new approach. And thus, we would start again.

LargeBank was now six months into its third transformation. This one was at a larger scale than the previous attempts, as it encompassed all of IT. The time frame was again two years. The budget was in the ballpark of $1 billion US. All the right transformational, Agile, and DevOps terms were being summarized at the meeting, and the internal presentations looked polished. However, having witnessed Nokia and then many other transformations that went sideways, and seeing the same pattern here yet again, I began to see a vision of $1 billion of the world's wealth being wasted without delivering a measurable improvement to value delivery.

To anyone with a Lean mind-set, that is a profoundly disturbing image, one that we want to do whatever we can to stop. That image got me mapping out the ideas for a framework that would make it possible for the business to understand what was going on and what was going wrong, and hopefully not repeat the same mistakes a fourth time. It was also that disturbing vision that got me to start writing this book, beginning with an article titled "How to Guarantee Failure in Your Agile DevOps Transformation" that I wrote immediately after the meeting.[9]

That third transformation effort has now concluded. The executives leading it were predictably removed once it looked like it was off track, as were the other IT and toolchain leaders who were involved. Again, I have had the opportunity to interview and learn from those who lasted long enough to witness how things after the transformation were worse for its key stakeholders than before the transformation started.

While I was sure at the outset that the transformation would fail to deliver a productivity increase, I was still shocked at hearing that it made things worse. I had thought that, with DevOps as a central component this third time around, there would be at least some successes, just not the promised business results. But in this case, from a value-delivery and talent-retention point of view, things got worse.

Wasting $1 billion of shareholder money or customer value should feel reprehensible, but a key premise of this book is that the leadership of the business and of IT would not have deliberately allowed that to happen. There is something fundamentally broken about the decision-making framework or organizational visibility that enables a business to get into this state over, and over, and over again.

A Disconnect between the Business and IT

To understand the lessons from LargeBank's transformation failure, we need a clearer picture of the business environment that enabled it. LargeBank is a successful financial-services institution, one forward-thinking enough to allocate a multi-billion-dollar budget to IT. It's an organization with a portfolio of thousands of applications and a desire to differentiate and compete on its digital assets, as evidenced by the organizational and budgetary commitment that it had to the transformation. In other words, from a strategic point of view, this organization positioned itself around the Age of Software much more than Nokia did. The CEO endorsed the transformation, but what was happening below the surface?

At LargeBank, IT is run as a cost center under the CFO. The business outcome that was being measured and managed was how much cost could be cut as a result of the transformation. At the outset, I did not see this as a fundamental problem, as so many of the organizations I work with are in a similar situation. However, after interviewing people involved with the transformation and hearing them discuss it, many of the unintended consequences appeared to point back to this as the source of the problem. For example, managing the cost alone meant that IT could run the transformation without closely involving the business stakeholders. If the goal is cost, who knows better than IT how to reduce infrastructure spending, staff costs, and other overheads?

On the business side, there were digital initiatives underway in parallel, with goals to design and create new digital experiences for mobile and web. However, these were divorced from the IT transformation—akin to building a great dashboard for a car without having a car or even a line of sight to a car that could support all of those fantastic new features. For example, other than proving a proof of concept in one part of the application portfolio for just one country or region. Due to this compartmentalization, it was impossible to know whether these mobile experiences could ever run on every type of system that the bank had across the globe.

The transformation was once again a local optimization of Large-Bank's value streams. On the IT side, it was focused on just the IT parts but not on the "value" parts; that is, those parts that needed to deliver value to the customers and to the business. On the digital side, it was ignoring the IT parts that would make the digital vision a reality, such as an architecture and delivery pipeline that could support the new user experiences envisioned. And the measurement of the transformation's success was cost reduction and adherence to the transformation project timelines rather than delivery of more business value at lower cost. In that sense, the outcome was predictable. Cost reduction would be achieved but at a significant reduction of the actual delivery capacity. This is a recipe for fumbling future survival through the Turning Point, as it leaves an open door for startups and tech giants to move in at the time of their choosing.

Lesson Two: If you manage a transformation according to cost alone, you will reduce productivity.

Falling into the Cost Center Trap

LargeBank's billion-dollar transformation project was functionally composed of countless subprojects, all of which were running to this two-year time frame. By virtue of being managed as projects, their goal was to be on time, on budget, and to deliver the business goal of cost reduction at the finish line. If every puzzle piece of this massive project fit perfectly with every other, and all were delivered on time and on budget, would that mean success? From an activity and project-oriented view, the answer is yes. But what about the business results? How were those measured at each step? How were bottlenecks identified across the tens of thousands of people, hundreds of processes, and dozens of tools? The bottom line is that they weren't.

Here, we find the root of the disconnect. When IT is treated as a cost center, the transformation takes on the same mentality. The focus becomes the successful reduction of cost at the end of the project time frame. Yet at the executive level, the very business case for the transformation would have touted the benefits of Agile and DevOps, such as faster time to market, more competitive product offerings, and more efficient delivery. However, those outcomes are not what gets measured by an organization that manages according to cost alone. While it's true that cost reduction can be a critical component of a transformation, that's not the issue. The issue is that a cost-centric framework did not deliver increased velocity, productivity, or efficiency, and instead resulted in the business getting a lot less for less instead of more for less.

Given the sophistication of LargeBank's transformation, more than cost metrics alone were used. The typical Agile transformation metrics, such as the number of teams following the Agile model, were also used, as were DevOps metrics, such as the number of deploys per day. But these are metrics of activities, not results. An IT team could be deploying a hundred times per day, but if their work intake is not connected to the needs of the business, the results will not materialize for the business. Once again, the proxy variables of "number of people trained on the Agile process" or "deploys per day" will only be meaningful if training or deployment are the bottleneck. But when the business is disconnected from IT, the Agile teams and DevOps pipeline never get the opportunity to become the bottleneck.

The problem is not the use of proxy metrics themselves; the problem is that we are relying on proxy metrics for decision making rather than finding the metrics that directly correspond to business outcomes. Consider Jeff Bezos's statement from his 2017 letter to shareholders in which he spoke, among other things, about resisting proxies:

Resist Proxies
As companies get larger and more complex, there's a tendency to manage to proxies. This comes in many shapes and sizes, and it's dangerous, subtle, and very Day 2.

A common example is process as proxy. Good process serves you so you can serve customers. But if you're not watchful, the process can become the thing. This can happen very easily in large organizations. The process becomes the proxy for the result you want. You stop looking at outcomes and just make sure you're doing the process right.[10]

In other parts of our business, we have outcome-based metrics, like revenue, daily active users, and Net Promoter Scores (NPS). The problem is that organizations do not have an agreed-upon set of metrics for measuring and tracking work in IT, and as such, settle for these proxies. And the wrong set of metrics is coming from measuring not the flow of value delivered but the "successful" execution of IT projects. In the next chapter, we will dive into the identification of a new outcome-based way of tracking value streams. But first, we need to further examine the origins and issues of the project-centric mentality as it applies to production.

From Puzzles to Planes

How is the approach at LargeBank so different from that of the BMW Group Leipzig plant? Is car production simpler somehow? Does it lend itself more easily to end-to-end measurement? How was the BMW Group able to transform how it builds cars so quickly, creating the i3 and i8 production lines without ever having mass produced electric cars or carbon-fiber bodies before? The BMW Group is just one example of the level of maturity, measurement, and adaptability that have been mastered in the Age of Mass Production.

Consider another highly complex artifact that epitomizes the Age of Mass Production. The Boeing 787 Dreamliner contains 2.3 million parts built in 5,400 factories.[11] Across all of its value streams, Boeing manages the production of 783 million parts across the hundreds of aircraft that it delivers each year.[12] It needs its products to stay relevant in the market for decades and bets the company on each new product introduction.

How is it that the BMW Group and Boeing can both manage existing production lines, transform their business to support new ones, and continually adapt to changes in technology, competition, and the market? The bottom line is that they are not stuck in the gridlocked puzzle pieces of project management. Instead, they have mastered a product-centric view of delivering value to their market.

My first exposure to this was a story told to me by Gail Murphy, then my professor in a third-year software engineering course, about the production of the Boeing 787's predecessor, the 777. The 777 was Boeing's first "fly-by-wire" plane. In other words, the software had to work, as it was purely software that was controlling the flaps and rudder and preventing the plane from falling out of the sky. Gail recounted that, due to the criticality of the software, Boeing decided to put all the heads of software engineering on the test flight. During the test flight, the plane started shaking, and the software engineers were able to implement a midflight fix via the turbulence control software.[13] I have yet to find a better example of an organization putting software leaders' skin in the game of high-stakes product development.

The depth of Boeing's understanding of the business implications of production and long-lived value streams is underscored by an event that unfolded during the production of their next plane, the 787 Dreamliner. The 787 Dreamliner project was Boeing's most ambitious to date and even more software-intensive than the 777. The Dreamliner was the first commercial plane to run on an electrical platform for everything ranging from cabin heating to wing ice protection, in comparison to previous commercial airlines that used much less efficient engine air-bleed systems.[14] In addition, Boeing decided to dramatically restructure its supply chain in order to lower the production costs of the plane—all while shifting to carbon-fiber wing and body parts. These and other complexities resulted in further delays.

In 2008, while following the program, I read of yet another delay, but the reason for this one seemed much more interesting. In this article, the general manager of the Dreamliner was quoted as saying: "It's not that the brakes do not work; it's the traceability of the software."[15]

This was fascinating to me—and not only because I was happy to read that the new plane would ship with functioning brakes. It was also intriguing to me because at the exact same time I was working on features in the Eclipse Mylyn open-source project to automate linking software requirements and defects to the lines of source code that had changed while developers worked on those items. For me, as well as my open-source colleagues at the time, the need to manually enter IDs to ensure traceability was tedious and error prone, and it was quite easy to automate since the Mylyn developer tool always knew what item the developer was working on.

Due to the hundreds of contributors on the Mylyn project, I required that every change to every line of code have traceability back to its originating feature or defect; otherwise, every time new work came in that was related to that code, we would have to manually search for why that code was there in the first place. That was far too tedious to do on such a resource-constrained project with millions of end users constantly submitting defects and requests, so I added a new feature to automate it. But why on earth would Boeing care about traceability to the extent of further risking the delivery time frames of the plane? Surely Boeing had a model that indicated an immense cost or risk for further delay. They could not possibly have the resource constraints that we were experiencing, so there must have been something more fundamental about their need for traceability.

In researching this further, I learned something even more fascinating. During a visit to Boeing, I remember learning that they design planes for approximately three decades of active production followed by another three decades of maintenance.[16] In other words, they are thinking ahead six decades in terms of support costs for both the hardware and the software. The brake software had been outsourced to General Electric, who, in turn, outsourced it to Hydro-Aire.[17] Hydro-Aire then delivered the working brake software using Subversion SCM, and provided General Electric and Boeing with both the source code and the binaries.[18] The software worked, passing the tests and meeting the requirements.[19] However, the source code did not have any traceability links to those requirements.[20] Adding traceability links after the fact is difficult and error prone. Given a sixty-year maintenance window and the overhead of compliance certifications, at a business level, Boeing knew that the most economical decision was to rewrite the brake software.

In spite of the Dreamliner's complexity and the scale of the transformation required to produce it, Boeing created an amazing product that has seen tremendous success in its market. What is it that Boeing understands about product development that so many IT organizations do not? How does Boeing think and plan beyond the typical one- or two-year project time frame to enable it to make such fundamental business decisions based on technical details? How do we get our organizations out of the fixed puzzle-piece mentality of enterprise

IT projects and into the excellence of production that we see in Boeing's and BMW Group's plants and organizations? How do we shift from project to product?

 Lesson Three: Engineering/IT and the business must be connected.

Toward Product Development Flow

If you've ever worked for a software startup, a tech giant, or a modern software vendor, you might be wondering what the fuss is all about. Of course, there is more to software products than minimizing costs; there are revenues, profits, active and delighted users, and all of those other metrics that populate objectives-and-key-results (OKR) systems. Tracking software delivery to business outcomes and treating it as a profit center is one of the main reasons why tech companies are faring so much better than their enterprise IT counterparts, who are stuck in what Mary Poppendieck calls the "cost center trap."[21]

Is this cost center approach endemic to large enterprise organizations? Consider how a large and very cost-conscious company like Boeing is managing the production of its Dreamliner. Costs are, of course, a key factor. But the success of Boeing depends not only on cost reduction but on the adoption and profitability of each plane for the span of its life cycle in the market—this is why Boeing innately takes a long view on the traceability of its software. Boeing knows that life cycle profitability will be affected if the software cannot be economically maintained, or if current or future regulation changes cannot be easily addressed in the software.

What Boeing demonstrates across its operations is that it treats its plane development as a profit center. The business sets goals, metrics, culture, and processes in a completely different direction than what we saw at LargeBank. I do not believe there is any less cost consciousness at Boeing, which continually works at reducing the production and supply-chain cost of every aircraft. But by doing so with an eye to revenue and profitability, an entirely different set of decisions can be made, like investing in the modularity of its value streams to modernize legacy offerings. A very visible example of that is the decision to modernize the 747, which first flew in 1969, with 787-style wings and engines to create the 747-8.[22]

As another example, consider what I witnessed at the BMW Group Leipzig plant. The scale of the 1- and 2-Series cars was impressive due to the massive automation and the seventy-second takt time (the rate at which a product step needs to be completed to meet customer demand). But what impressed me even more was the very different way that the i3 and i8 lines were set up, as I will recount in an upcoming story.

The market adoption and profitability of the BMW Group's electric cars would be hard to determine in a changing market, so the BMW Group created a production architecture to support learning from the market before investing further in automation of the lines. The profitability and product/market fit drove the architecture of the value stream, not vice versa. Again, it was a complete one-eighty from the approach at LargeBank, where IT was transforming for IT's sake. The production infrastructure, architecture, and managerial approach could not be more starkly different. That was the point that hit home when I visited both LargeBank and the BMW Group on the same trip, and was flying home with my head pressed against the window of a Boeing Dreamliner.

To those who have studied the concepts of Donald Reinertsen's *Product Development Flow*, none of this will be news. Reinertsen makes a very clear and compelling case for throwing out proxy variables and measuring for a singular economic objective: life cycle profits.[23] However, depending on where in the company or product maturity curve your focus is, this objective might change.

In *Zone to Win*, Moore provides a model with four distinct investment zones (Figure 2.3).[24] The *Productivity Zone* is focused on making the bottom line and includes systems such as HR and marketing. The *Performance Zone* is about the top line and includes the main drivers of revenue. The *Incubation Zone* is where new products and businesses are developed before just one or the other is moved into the *Transformation Zone* and used to play disruption offence or defense. In defining a value metric for different product lines, the zone and its goals must be identified. For example, in the Incubation Zone, the business objective might be monthly active users, before transitioning to a Transformation Zone where the focus is more on revenue than on profit (Figure 2.3).

The mistakes many organizations are making in their digital transformations are in using the metrics from the Productivity Zone—costs and the bottom line—for measuring their entire IT and software delivery capabilities. Prior to the Age of Software, all of IT could be relegated to the Productivity Zone; but the whole purpose of a digital transformation is to allow the organization to launch and manage products in the other zones, which is what will determine their future relevance in the market.

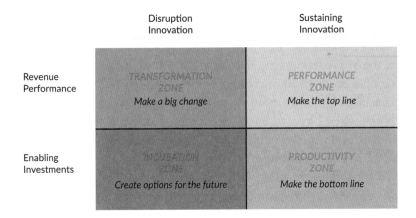

Figure 2.3: Zone Management[25]

Projects versus Products

Project management is a practice that has enabled some of the world's most visible and impressive accomplishments. It has been iconified by the Gantt chart, created by Henry Gantt in 1917 and subsequently used to build the Hoover Dam, the largest concrete construction of its time. This was the tail end of the Deployment Period of the Age of Steel, during which the practices of Taylorism were adopted in order to improve and scale labor efficiency. Those practices provided a way of creating standard work processes and best practices, as well as the specialization and division of labor at scale.

While it may not have been Taylor's intent, when put to practice by others, Taylorism assumed that people could be treated as interchangeable resources that could be assigned and reassigned to projects. Such treatment of workers as machines is not only dehumanizing but also shortsighted, as later demonstrated by Henry Ford, who realized the importance of decentralized decision making and autonomy.

These problems are so fundamental that the Age of Mass Production was, in part, catalyzed by the methods applied by Ford. Fordism put significantly more emphasis on the actual worker, their training, and their economic well-being.[26] The companies that excelled in the Age of Mass Production built on Fordism and extended it with approaches that further connected production to the business, such as Toyota's innovation of the Andon cord.[27]

The effectiveness of this is exactly what the walk through the BMW Group Leipzig plant identified. What that journey led me to conclude is that many enterprise IT organizations are still managing to the project-oriented world of Taylorism from the Age of Steel. This disconnect is what is causing the massive communication gap between business leaders and technologists.

Software delivery is, by its nature, creative work. Software specialists are skilled at automating repetitive processes when given the chance, leaving only the complex work and decision making that humans continue to excel at. Applying management frameworks from a hundred years ago to organizations that need to compete on digital assets is futile. To make this more concrete, Table 2.1 contrasts a project-oriented approach with a product-oriented one.

Budgeting

One of the most important aspects of structuring IT and software investments is budgeting, as budgeting has such an influence on organizational behavior. The budgeting of projects assumes a high degree of market and resource certainty, as it creates a fixed end goal and measures success to being on time and on budget. It also creates an incentive for stakeholders to ask for as large a budget as possible, since the budget has to factor in any uncertainty to the project time frames. In addition, going back for more budget requires significant effort or the creation of a new project.

	Project-Oriented Management	Product-Oriented Management
Budgeting	Funding of milestones, pre-defined at project scoping. New budget requires creation of a new project.	Funding of product value streams based on business results. New budget allocation based on demand. Incentive to deliver incremental results.
Time Frames	Term of the project (e.g., one year). Defined end date. Not focused on the maintenance/health after the project ends.	Life cycle of the product (multiple years), includes ongoing health/maintenance activities through end of life.
Success	Cost center approach. Measured to being on time and on budget. Capitalization of development results in large projects. Business incentivised to ask for everything they might need up front.	Profit center approach. Measured in business objectives and outcomes met (e.g., revenue). Focus on incremental value delivery and regular checkpoint.
Risk	Delivery risks, such as product/market fit, is maximized by forcing all learning, specification, and strategic decision making to occur up front.	Risk is spread across the time frame and iterations of the project. This creates option value, such as terminating the project if delivery assumptions were incorrect or pivoting if strategic opportunities arise.
Teams	Bring people to the work: allocated up front, people often span multiple projects, frequent churn and re-assignment.	Bring work to the people: stable, incrementally adjusted, cross-functional teams assigned to one value stream.
Prioritization	PPM and project plan driven. Focus on requirements delivery. Projects drive waterfall orientation.	Roadmap and hypothesis testing driven. Focus on feature and business value delivery. Products drive Agile orientation.
Visibility	IT is a black box. PMOs create complex mapping and obscurity.	Direct mapping to business outcomes, enabling transparency.

Table 2.1: Project-Oriented Management vs. Product-Oriented Management

This is where the mismatch becomes immediately apparent. DevOps and Agile are all about creating a feedback loop to address the inherent uncertainty of software delivery and then providing the feedback loop to the business to adjust accordingly. The more certainty there is, the more optimal a long-term allocation of resources gets created by a project plan. However, due to the degree of complexity in software delivery and the inherent rate of change in the market due to the Turning Point, baking all that uncertainty into project plans not only creates tremendous waste but gives the business visibility into the wrong things, providing a view into activities and proxy metrics over visibility into the incremental delivery of business results.

In an Incubation or Transformation Zone initiative, there could be more uncertainty than certainty. This results in project plans that incentivize delaying releases and customer testing in order to implement everything that was needed at the start of the project. And this multiplies the product/market-fit (PMF) risk by removing the possibility of iterative learning from the market and pivoting accordingly.

In contrast, product-oriented management focuses on measuring the results of each unit of investment that brings value to the business. Those units are products; they deliver value to a customer, and as such, the measurement must be based on those business outcomes. Funding of new value streams is based on a business case for that product, as is ongoing investment in those value streams.

The approach need not be disruptive to the annual planning cycle. For example, at Tasktop we create annual budgets for the product and engineering departments that are signed off by our board; but every quarter we review the allocation of those budgets to the products' value streams (e.g., staffing up a promising new Incubation Zone offering once it has customer validation).

More aggressive Lean Budget approaches have also been proposed, to more quickly respond to cost overruns or revenue opportunities for a particular value stream. Whether an annual or a more frequent budgeting cycle is used, what's important is that products, not projects, are the unit of investment.

Time Frames

One of the biggest problems that project-oriented management faces stems from the consideration of time frames. A project has a defined time frame after which resources ramp down. This makes perfect sense when building a skyscraper, as there is a definitive and well-understood end to the project: after the skyscraper is erected, the project moves into a maintenance period. However, products, be they software or hardware, have a life cycle, not a definitive end. Products can be end-of-lifed; for example, Google has killed dozens of products, including Google Reader and Google Wave. As long as a product is available, defect fixes and new features are requested, as the ecosystem around software products is constantly evolving.

Applying the project-oriented mentality of creating then launching a software product, and then assuming it can be reduced to a fraction of its investment when in maintenance mode, has many unintended consequences. For example, one enterprise organization that I worked with did a survey to assess the state of project management across thousands of IT staff. They found that the number of projects that an engineer was assigned to over the course of a year ranged from six to twelve on average, depending on where they worked in the organization.

I personally went through this in the early days of Tasktop, allocating people and teams to multiple open-source services projects. I noticed a dramatic productivity reduction when an engineer was assigned to more than a single value stream. This staffing antipattern comes from the annual allocation of people to projects and the assumptions that the projects will not require much work during maintenance, leaving people with the impression that it will only take a small slice of any given person's time. The reality is that if the product is used, the need to do fixes is regular, and as I witnessed, the thrashing becomes a major drag on both happiness and productivity.

Some organizations address the post-project maintenance of software by outsourcing it to organizations such as the global systems integrator (GSI). This additionally reduces the apparent cost of maintaining the software, potentially removing it as a liability on the balance sheet. This outsourcing appears to work in theory, but it can cripple flow and feedback loops, as organizational boundaries need to be crossed. In addition, it further disconnects that software from the business. If the software was core to the business, this is debilitating in terms of continuing to deliver business results, as the need for change and updates is constant in software.

The false notion of a software project's end is also wrong from an economic point of view. Some of the perceived economic benefits will be removed with the implementation of IFRS (International Financial Reporting Standards) revenue recognition rules in the US, which may also remove the balance sheet bias toward outsourcing. But in product-oriented management, the focus needs to be on life cycle costs and profitability, as exemplified by the Boeing example earlier.

It gets worse. With this "project-end fallacy," key aspects of the economics of software delivery are not visible to the organization. For example, one of the core concepts that we will review in the next chapter is technical debt. The accumulation of technical debt that results from normal software development creates problems that are well documented. And if this debt is not reduced regularly, the software becomes prohibitively difficult and expensive to add features to or to fix.

This was a key part of the failure that we saw in Nokia's story, where technical debt contributed to the loss of the mobile market that it dominated. In project-oriented management, there is no incentive to reduce technical debt; its effects do not materialize until after the project ends. This results in application portfolios that are dead ends for the companies that created them and in the constant accumulation of more legacy systems and code.

Success

At a leadership level, the success metrics that we place on our organizations and on our teams will determine behavior. Project-oriented management tends to take a cost center approach, which is still common for enterprise IT. As we witnessed with the story of LargeBank, expecting an increase in the delivery of business value from a cost center is pointless.

Project-oriented management also brings with it some side effects that go against the principles of DevOps. For example, the capitalization of software development results in an incentive to create large projects. Stakeholders are incentivized to ask up front for everything that might be needed during the course of the project, which goes directly against Lean thinking and continual learning. The companies who are navigating the Turning Point measure software investment in terms of business outcomes, like internal adoption or revenue generation. This results in a fast-learning managerial culture of incremental value delivery and regular checkpoints.

As Figure 2.4 depicts, product orientation enables an alignment of the organization to business outcomes, not functional silos.

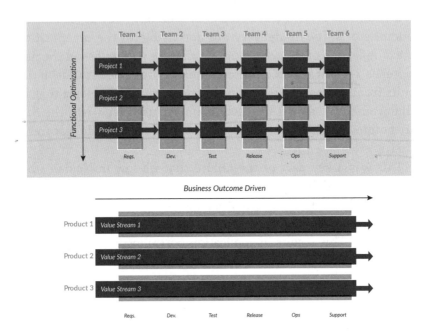

Figure 2.4: Functional Optimization vs. Business Outcomes

Risk

Project-oriented management is designed to identify and create contingencies for all risks that could be incurred during the project. However, that requires up-front knowledge of all the risks, which works in some domains but not in the highly uncertain and changing world of software delivery.

The Cynefin framework provides a taxonomy of decision-making contexts, including obvious, complicated, complex, and chaotic.[28] Due to the rate of change in technology stacks and in the market, software initiatives tend to fall into the complex or chaotic zone. As a result, project-oriented management, which is optimized for the obvious and the complicated contexts, ends up padding projects for any contingencies that may come up during the project's time frame. This results in overly conservative time frames and inflated budgets. But not even those can stave off product market risk, where any up-front planning is less effective than regular hypothesis testing and learning.

In contrast, Lean Startup and approaches such as minimum viable products (MVPs), are a key part of the product-oriented mind-set. In addition to reducing risk, the incremental product-oriented approach creates option value by allowing the business to pivot at regular checkpoints. This is not without an overhead, as the more frequent reviews and checkpoints require expensive managerial bandwidth. But due to the complexity of software and the rate of change in the market, this overhead is best spread out across a product life cycle rather than incurred at project inception and again at failure.

Teams

With project-oriented management, resources are allocated to projects. This follows the Taylorist philosophy that people are fungible and expendable. That assumption breaks down completely in software delivery, which is one of the most complex disciplines of knowledge work.

Modern software value streams are built on millions or tens of millions of lines of code. At Tasktop, the most complex part of our codebase takes a senior and highly experienced developer six months to ramp up to full productivity. Consider the productivity impact of allocating people to new projects every twelve months. Unfortunately, this is not far from the norm, as most enterprise IT organizations do not model or measure developer productivity, engagement, or ramp-up time; and with a Taylorist mind-set, are unaware of the overheads.

Overlaid on top of the costs to the individual IT specialist's productivity and happiness are the costs to the team. Teams working on complex problems go through what psychologist Bruce Tuckman coined the forming, storming, norming, and performing life cycle.[29] Reallocating people disrupts that cycle; the more people are moved, the higher the productivity cost for the team.

The project-oriented management approach of "bringing people to work" is not suited for complex knowledge work, like software delivery. High-performing software organizations have already learned that "bringing work to people" is more effective. Long-lived teams allow for expertise (both individual and team) and relationships to build over time, improving both velocity and morale. This enables other benefits as well, such as problems being solved at the lowest level of the organization instead of having the nonscalable, constant escalations to management that result from changes to plan.

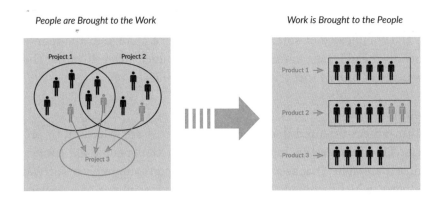

Figure 2.5: Bringing the People to the Work vs. Work to the People

In large-scale software, the optimal allocation is a one-to-one allocation between teams and value streams in order to maximize team and expertise building. The adoption of *feature teams* is one example of this kind of allocation, though value streams for larger products will often consist of multiple feature teams.

Prioritization

In project-oriented management, the project plan drives priorities. Changes to the plan are expensive in terms of management overhead, communication, and coordination; and as such, adjustments to the plan tend to be minimized. In software delivery terms, this tends to drive a "waterfall" software delivery model, as that is the model that naturally aligns to a cascading project plan. While this is suitable to projects with a high degree of predictability, it is counterproductive for software delivery. Product-oriented management sets priorities based on product road maps of features and constant hypothesis testing. At an organizational level, this means applying the feedback and continual learning principles of DevOps at all levels of the organization, right up to senior management.

Visibility

Last and perhaps most important is the problem of visibility. In the Nokia and LargeBank examples we reviewed earlier in this chapter, the common theme is the disconnect between the business and IT. What is the source of the disconnect? Given that the leadership and business representatives have such a broad purview, how is it possible that there is a lack of visibility into IT? In a time when we have ubiquitous access to big data and analytics tools, how can IT feel like a black box at so many organizations?

The problem is not due to data access; the problem results from a mismatch of the data models with which IT works and with which the business is operating. IT and software delivery professionals already work and think in product-oriented mind-sets and methodologies. That is what the business has tasked them to do—to deliver value through software offerings. However, if the business side is still thinking and managing in terms of projects, constant mapping and remapping needs to be done between the more iterative nature of software delivery and the more static nature of techniques, such as project and portfolio management and earned-value management.

The end result is the "watermelon" phenomenon.[30] When engineering leads are asked by project managers if they are on track, the answer is yes, because the question is ambiguous. Once the release plays itself out and business goals are not met, it is clear that the projects were not on track. The projects were "green" on the outside and "red" on the inside (like a watermelon). But the problem is not with the projects; instead, it is with the management paradigm that was never designed to handle the complexity and dynamics of software delivery.

Conclusion

Marked by a project-over-product mentality, an emphasis on cost over profit, and adherence to time frames over delivery of business value, this disconnect between the business and IT is at the core of IT and digital transformation failures. This is what our organizations need to learn from the last Deployment Period in order to have a shot at competing against the upstarts of the current one and set the foundation to thrive in the next decade.

The challenge is that, at enterprise IT scale, we have not had the management framework nor the infrastructure needed to manage large-scale software product delivery. As you will discover in the next chapter, the Flow Framework provides a new approach to managing software delivery to business results instead of technical activities.

The goal of the Flow Framework is to provide the missing layer between business-driven digital transformations and the technical transformations that underpin them. If the digital transformation is focused on processes and activities instead of business results, it is unlikely to succeed; and the business is unlikely to realize that until it is too late. The concepts of organizational charts and Scrum teams will continue to be as relevant as ever. But for an organization wanting to become a software innovator, these are secondary to product-oriented value streams. The Flow Framework ensures that your transformation is grounded in connecting, measuring, and managing your Value Stream Network, which is the critical layer needed to succeed with software delivery at scale.

Neither the shift to a product-oriented management nor the Flow Framework are sufficient to assure success in the Age of Software. Organizations need a managerial culture and understanding of a rapidly changing market in order to bring software-based products to market and adapt. But before we consider how to deliver more value, we must first define how we measure business value in software delivery. That is where the Flow Framework comes in.

CHAPTER 3

Introducing the Flow Framework

What we have discovered so far is that enterprise organizations are attempting to use managerial mechanisms from previous ages to direct software delivery in this one. IT and software delivery costs have been growing for decades, yet our organizations do not have adequate visibility or understanding of what is now one of the largest costs of doing business. Meanwhile, the tech giants and digital startups have already mastered the managerial frameworks necessary to succeed in the Age of Software. So have many of the technologists working within enterprises, and these technologists are pushing hard on their organizations to deploy the DevOps and Agile practices that they know are critical to transformation.

The problem is that the principles of modern software-delivery approaches are not translating to the business. For example, enterprises are still managing IT as a set of projects or a cost center, rather than taking the product-oriented mentality that defined the winners of the Age of Mass Production.

We need our businesses to adapt to this product-oriented mind-set and to do so in a way that supports the vast differences between producing physical widgets and infinitely malleable software components. We need a new framework, one that elevates the best practices of Agile and Lean frameworks to the business. We need to define business outcome–oriented metrics instead of relying on activity-oriented proxy metrics.

In this chapter, I introduce the Flow Framework as a new approach for connecting the business to technology. The Flow Framework is not intended to help you spot market shifts or strategize offerings that will disintermediate disruptors; it is intended to provide you with a layer that bridges the gap between business strategy and technology delivery. The Flow Framework opens up the black box of IT so you can create an organization-wide feedback loop, accelerating the flow of business value to customers and the organizational learning to adapt as the market continues through the second half of the Age of Software.

To support the deployment of the Flow Framework, this chapter introduces Value Stream Networks as the key infrastructure concept needed to bring about the same kind of automation and visibility for software delivery that we see in manufacturing. The chapter concludes with an overview of the Flow Framework and a definition of the four flow items that are at its core. But before we learn more, let's revisit the plant.

BMW TRIP Walking the Lines

Looking down at the 1- and 2-Series production process in action, it is hard not to marvel at the choreographed actions of the robots and blue-vested production-line workers. We walk about a mile around the Assembly Building, slowing down to examine the various workstations. Some are fully automated, with large robots welding, assembling, and gluing. Others have workers performing intricate assembly steps. Frank stops us at a particularly intricate part of the line, pointing out some wiring harnesses and describing how each of these will form the electrical nervous system of the car.

"Every single harness is different," Frank says. "Each car is made to order, which means countless combinations of options for electronic components. Because of this, each wiring harness is assembled specifically for that car prior to arrival at the line."

Frank describes just how complex harness fitting on the production line is. He explains that if something goes wrong with the installation and it does not finish in the takt time of seventy seconds, a cord is pulled; then, assistance can come from the next workstation to complete the job. The production line is structured to ensure this highly complex job is completed reliably, without having to remove cars from the line for rework.

Frank explains how complicated it would be to pull a car off the line at this point, because there are still miles of production line downstream. Every single workstation would need to compensate for the resequencing of the flow of parts. As such, many additional steps and processes are in place to avoid removing a car from the flow.

I'm struck by the parallel between this and what happens when a software team breaks a build due to working out of sync with the latest code, and just how expensive that scenario is for a software organization. Here, everything is synchronized to ensure continuous flow, including the slack needed if a worker cannot complete the harness install in time.

Further along the line are the "knuckles"—the parts of the building where the line takes a ninety-degree turn to the left, proceeds into the "finger" building (which looks like an endless corridor of additional assembly steps), then returns to where we are standing before proceeding to the next finger.

"Sunroof installation is so complex that we never want to move this workstation," Frank says. "The robots are bolted right into the floor, unlike the other stations, where they can be moved. Now you see why the building has this architecture. We can extend the fingers with new manufacturing steps, but the knuckles themselves are the fixed points in the production line."

The entire physical architecture of the plant has been optimized around the current and potential future flow along the line. The five knuckles are the most complex parts of the value stream, which is why the buildings are built around them—to maximize flow and future extensibility within these key constraints of the line's value stream architecture.

Why could we not think with this kind of high-level clarity about constraints and dependencies in software delivery? Why is it that we architect around technology boundaries and not around value stream flow?

Why We Need a New Framework

The transformation challenges outlined in Part I are fundamental. Doing something about them is not required, and many companies will end up staying the course in their ineffective approach to managing software delivery. Today, definitive data exists to determine how quickly the next disruptions will happen, or which approach or framework is most effective at addressing them.

By the time data is available to analysts and researchers it will be too late. The winners and losers of the Age of Software will have gained enough market share that those applying management techniques of previous ages will find it difficult or impossible to catch up without regulation or other forms of government intervention. We see signs of this already: whenever Amazon's share price goes up, the share price of retailers like Target, Walmart, and Nordstrom's goes down;[1] and vice versa. This does not represent typical market dynamics. We are seeing a zero-sum game that will keep playing itself out industry by industry as we continue to head through the Turning Point.

Numerous methodologies and frameworks exist for transforming, modernizing, and reengineering every aspect of your business. Some, like the Scaled Agile Framework (SAFe), are focused on enterprise software delivery. Recent advances in DevOps practices address bottlenecks in how software is built and released. Other frameworks, like Moore's Zone Management, address transformation from a business reengineering point of view.

Such practices and frameworks are as relevant as ever, and the Flow Framework assumes that the best-suited practices for your business are already underway. The role of the Flow Framework is to ensure that the business-level frameworks and transformation initiatives are connected to the technical ones. It is the isolation of these initiatives that is causing so many transformations to stall or to fail.

To achieve the Three Ways of DevOps—flow, feedback, and continuous learning—we need to scale the ways of DevOps beyond IT to the business. We need a new framework to plan, monitor, and ensure the success of today's software-centric digital transformations. This new framework cannot be separate from the business; it must be connected directly to the measurement of business objectives and key results. It also cannot ignore the idiosyncrasies of software development or assume that software can be managed like manufacturing. And it cannot be overly focused on one aspect of software delivery, be that development, operations, or customer success.

The new framework must encapsulate the management of large-scale software delivery in a similar way to how value stream mapping, enterprise-request processing, and supply-chain management provided the managerial building blocks needed to master manufacturing. This is the role of the Flow Framework.

At the Leipzig plant, all staff know who the customer is. All staff can see the activity of the company's value streams along the production lines. All staff know what business the customer pulls from those value streams: cars that deliver on BMW's mantra of "Sheer Driving Pleasure." And all staff know what the plant's bottleneck is. Contrast that to today's enterprise IT organizations, where not just the staff but the leadership have problems answering the questions most fundamental to production:

- Who is the customer?
- What value is the customer pulling?
- What are the value streams?
- Where is the bottleneck?

For example, at LargeBank, the delivery efforts were not structured into products supported by value streams, so there was no clear or consistent way of identifying the customer for each part of the project portfolio. For many internal applications and components, the customer was not specified; and in many cases, delivery was more closely aligned to legacy software architecture than to internal or external customer pull. Extracting the value streams from project-oriented management was impossible due to all of the overlap between the projects and a lack of alignment between the projects and the software architecture. And due to all the disparate systems and focus on local optimization and tracking of activities instead of results, it was impossible for anyone to reliably know where the bottleneck was.

The Flow Framework provides a simple path to answering these questions. There are key staff within your organization who already know the answers, but their efforts and vision need to be connected to an organizational strategy and approach. Most important, it provides you with a way of connecting your Value Stream Network, measuring the flow of business value and correlating that to your strategy and business outcomes. The Flow Framework will allow you to:

- See the end-to-end flow of business value in real time
- Instantly spot bottlenecks and use them to prioritize investment
- Test hypotheses based on real-time data from every value stream
- Rearchitect your organization around maximizing flow

A digital organization that competes without a connected and visible Value Stream Network will become akin to a manufacturer trying to compete in the last age without an electrical network. These organizations will learn that managing IT without flow metrics or something equivalent is like managing a cloud infrastructure without a mechanism for measuring the cost of electricity and computer power.

Focus on End-to-End Results

Organizational charts and enterprise architecture are the best representations of value creation that we have; but they are failing us, and we know it. Software investment and staffing decisions are made anecdotally, using static and stale pieces of data and activity-based proxies for business value rather than metrics that directly correlate technology investments with business results.

At the BMW Group Leipzig plant, the flow of value was clear and visible. Units of value—the cars—flowed along assembly to final production. The velocity of delivery and the quality and completeness of each unit could be inspected individually and in aggregate. In software organizations, we do not have the benefit of tangible and visible objects flowing through a production line.

unit of value = the segment

Define metrics (value)
By train

But what if we did? What if we could take a real-time, animated MRI of the software organization? What would we see flowing from the business to the customer? What patterns would we see in the flow? Could we spot the bottlenecks where flow is impeded? These are the questions the Flow Framework answers.

The Flow Framework provides a system for the end-to-end measurement of the results of software delivery. The focus is on the measurement of the ground truth of software delivery—the actual work being done—and connecting the work to results, such as revenue generation. The focus is entirely on result-oriented business metrics, like revenue and cost, not proxy metrics for value creation, like lines of code created or deploys per day.

This is not to say that proxy metrics of that sort are not important. For example, if lack of continuous delivery automation is the bottleneck for a value stream, then measuring deploys per day becomes a critical metric. However, the Flow Framework is focused on the end-to-end metrics used to identify bottlenecks wherever they lie in the value stream. In addition, the Flow Framework avoids measures of activity in favor of results. There are no metrics of "how Agile" a team or organization is; there's just a focus on how much business value flows. If Agile development is a bottleneck, then measuring a proxy such as the number of people trained on Scrum can result in an increase to the flow of business value.

But the role of the Flow Framework is not to specify how to achieve agility; that is the role of Agile frameworks and training programs. The role of the Flow Framework is to help you track, manage, and improve your investments in automation and agility.

Lean Thinking Required

While the Flow Framework does not require the implementation of a specific Agile framework or working model, nor any specific approach to DevOps or customer success, it does require a commitment to the Lean concepts that are the foundation of those approaches. At the highest level, the purpose of the Flow Framework is to provide an actionable way of implementing the concepts of Lean thinking for large-scale software delivery. Those concepts are defined by James P. Womack and Daniel T. Jones in their *Lean Thinking* book as follows:

> . . . lean thinking can be summarized in five principles: precisely specify value by specific product, identify the value stream for each product, make value flow without interruptions, let the customer pull value from the producer, and pursue perfection.[2]

The Flow Framework requires a business-level commitment to product and value stream thinking, and the principles of flow and customer pull that underpin Lean thinking. As we move through this book, we will identify these five principles with an emphasis on how they relate to managing software delivery. To do that, we must first precisely define how these concepts of flow, pull, and value streams translate from the Age of Mass Production to the Age of Software.

What Is a Value Stream?

One of the first principles in Lean thinking is to "identify the value stream for each product."[3] We will go into detail on how we do that in Chapter 9; for now, consider it to include every person, process, activity, and tool related to delivering that software product.

> **Value Stream:** The end-to-end set of activities performed to deliver value to a customer through a product or service.

Each product needs to be well defined as a packaging of software features that a customer uses, either directly or embedded as part of another physical or digital offering. That means the customer needs to be well defined too, but the customer need not be defined strictly as an external user. For example, an internal business user of a billing system is also a customer, meaning that the billing system can and should have its own value stream. Some organizations may have a team that produces an internal platform or API (application programming interface) that is only consumed by other developers within the organization. In that case, the customers are the consumers of that API.

Define Customer by product

Each product has a customer who consumes the software produced by that product's value stream.

Value streams are composed of all the activities, stakeholders, processes, and tools required to deliver business value to the customer. While this may sound obvious, my second epiphany was all about the fact that instead of creating abstractions around end-to-end value streams, organizations keep creating them within functional silos. For instance, if support teams or business stakeholders are excluded from the process, the result is no longer a value stream but a segment of the value stream. As such, Agile teams are segments of the value stream, as are DevOps teams. Even cross-functional feature teams rarely constitute the full value stream at a large organization. For example, as they tend to exclude the support team.

This is not to say that value stream segments are not important, only that managing and measuring them is not the topic of this book. The practices we have around the various segments are mature when compared to how organizations are approaching end-to-end value streams. For example, many enterprise IT organizations are using robust combinations of requirements management, project and portfolio management, enterprise Agile, continuous delivery and DevOps, ITIL, and customer success. Each has multiple frameworks, tools, and metrics that are continuing to evolve. The Flow Framework states that we need a new practice for managing end-to-end value streams in a similar way to how value stream mapping gave the Age of Mass Production the boost it needed to master large-scale delivery of physical products.

From Mapping to Architecture

As manufacturing matured throughout the Age of Mass Production, best practices formed to handle the complexity and management of the end-to-end process. A key practice in manufacturing plant operations is value stream mapping, as summarized by Mike Rother and John Shook in *Learning to See*.[4] This practice provides a visual notation and set of metrics for the management of production flows and the identification of waste and bottlenecks in production systems. An example of a value stream map can be found in Figure 3.1, where we can see how production is mapped out to support a customer pulling widgets through a manufacturing flow. We need a similar way of understanding, architecting, and optimizing the flow of business value in large-scale software delivery.

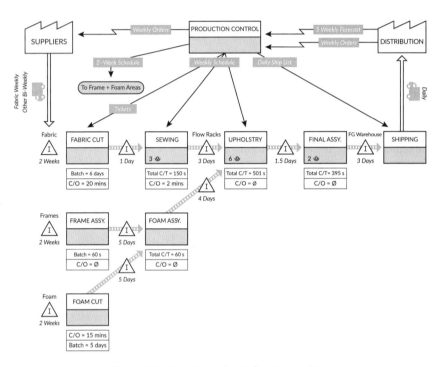

Figure 3.1: Manufacturing Value Stream Map

Finding Flow in Software Delivery

The Flow Framework started with my attempt to visualize manufacturing like production flow for software delivery. The core premise of the Flow Framework is that we need to measure the end-to-end flow of business value. If we measure a subset of the flow, such as the time it takes for developers to complete an Agile "user story" or the time it takes to deploy software, we can only optimize a segment of the value stream. The goal of the Flow Framework is an end-to-end view that

not a SEGMENT eg Search

we can correlate to business results. As such, the top level of the Flow Framework only focuses on how end-to-end flow items and metrics are correlated to business outcomes. The definition of flow is similar to what we know from manufacturing, but it is specific to what flows through a software delivery process.

> *Software Flow:* *The activities involved in producing business value along a software value stream.*

The Flow Framework focuses entirely on the end-to-end value stream flow and its correlation to business results (Figure 3.2). The measurement is done via the ground truth of software delivery that is observed by the flow of artifacts through the Value Stream Network (as detailed in Part III). Agile and DevOps metrics and telemetry lie a layer down below the Flow Framework. For example, if an Agile team is constantly struggling with meeting its release goals, the SAFe or Scrum frameworks can provide metrics and guidelines for better prioritization and planning. In contrast, the Flow Framework is focused on the end-to-end metrics used to identify where those bottlenecks might lie in the first place—if they ECS? are upstream or downstream of development, for instance.

In addition, the Flow Framework avoids measures of activity in favor NB of tracking flow metrics and correlating them to results. There are no metrics of "how Agile" or "how DevOps" an organization is, just a focus on how much business value flows through each value stream and what results it produces. If responsiveness to the market is a key need, the Flow Framework can highlight flow and feedback cycles that are too slow for a particular value, implying that more Agile practices may be needed.

The role of the Flow Framework is to help you determine the outcomes of your investments in Agile and DevOps practices, and to supply you with the metrics needed to improve those practices. In summary, the goal is to provide you with a means of scaling flow, feedback, and continual learning to work not just for Dev and Ops but for the end-to-end business process of software delivery.

At the top level, the Flow Framework provides two things. First, the Value Stream Metrics allow you to track each value stream within the organization so that you have a way of correlating production metrics to business outcomes. Second, the Value Stream Network layer provides the infrastructure needed to measure the results delivered by each product.

At the highest level, the Flow Framework is a mechanism for aligning all delivery activities in your organization around your software products, tracking the business results of those activities in order to create a results-driven feedback loop.

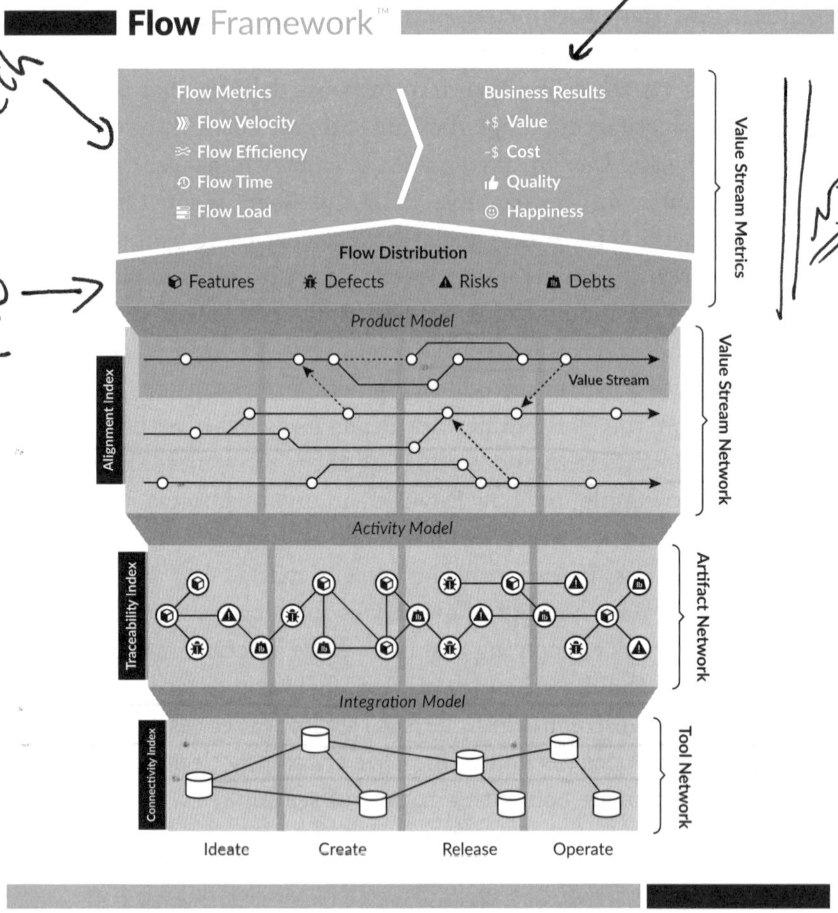

Figure 3.2: The Flow Framework

To do that, we must switch to first principles and define the customer, what they are pulling, and how this pull can be implemented as value stream flow. Once one or more value streams are defined, we need to focus on making value(s) flow smoothly across those value streams. But before we do that, we must define the units that flow along a software value stream.

The Flow Framework is designed to work at the largest of organizational scales and to support stringent regulatory requirements where needed (discussed in Part III). This means that even the most traditional, complex, or safety-critical organizations can apply the concepts to drive software innovation at the right pace for their business. In order to do this, we first need to understand the four main flow items that make up the framework.

The Four Flow Items

Every time that I have asked a senior- or executive-level IT leader where their bottleneck is, I have received either a blank stare or a vague answer. But when set in the right context, just the thought process of exploring this question makes a serious issue apparent. The vast majority of enterprise IT organizations do not have a well-defined productivity measure for what flows in their software production process.

It is impossible for the business to have a shared understanding of a bottleneck without having a shared understanding of productivity. Contrast that to the automotive industry, where the number of cars produced is a very clear productivity measure of an automotive value stream. Worse yet, it's not just those organizations that are scrambling to align around metrics that matter; it's the software industry as a whole.

There is no clear consensus from academia or from industry thought leaders on what constitutes software development productivity. Organizations know it when they see it—perhaps through products that drive market adoption and revenue faster than others. But correlating development activities to those results has been more of an opaque art than a disciplined activity. To define productivity in a value stream, we must first define what flows.

Do ~~the~~ our products have indirect monetization?

To do that, we need to go back to the first principles of Lean thinking summarized earlier in this chapter. Lean thinking starts not with the product but with the value the customer pulls. If we think back to the early days of software, with companies stamping out installer disks packaged in shrink-wrapped boxes, we could try to draw an analogy to car production and define the widgets produced as those boxes. But that analogy was weak then and is rendered irrelevant in this time of continuous delivery and the cloud. If customers are not pulling releases, what value does the customer pull?

Efficiency? Segment?
To pull value, the customer must be able to see that value and be willing to exchange some economic unit for it. For an internal product, this could be adoption (e.g., having different business units adopt a common authentication system). For an external product, the unit can be revenue; or in the case of a product with indirect or ad-based monetization, such as a social media tool, it might be time engaged with the product. For a government or not-for-profit organization, it can be the adoption rate of a newly-launched digital offering.

Using any of these scenarios, consider the last time you derived new value from a product or went back to using a product that you had previously not used. What triggered that exchange of value in terms of spending your time or your money? Chances are that it was a new feature that met your usage needs and perhaps delighted you in some way. Or it was the fix for a defect that was preventing you from using a product that you had otherwise valued. And here lies the key to defining what flows in a software value stream: if what we are pulling is new features and defect fixes, those are the flow items of a software value stream.

NB

> **Flow Item:** A unit of business value pulled by a stakeholder through a product's value stream.

If these are the flow items, that means we could characterize work across all the people and teams within a value stream as applying to one of these items—and we can. Given full visibility into every process and tool in the organization, you could identify exactly how many designers, developers, managers, testers, and help-desk professionals were

↳ is flow features + bug fixes?!

involved with creating, deploying, and supporting a particular feature. The same goes for a defect. But is this the only work that is being done within the value streams?

The "Mining the Ground Truth of Enterprise Toolchains" analysis of 308 enterprise IT tool networks (the study I noted in Chapter 1) identified two other kinds of work that are invisible to the user but are pulled through the value stream by a different kind of stakeholder.[5] First, there is work on risks. This includes the various kinds of security, regulation, and compliance that must be defined by business analysts, scheduled onto development backlogs, implemented, tested, deployed, and maintained. In other words, this is work that competes for priority over features and defects, and as such, is one of the primary flow items. This type of work is not pulled by the customer, as regulatory- or compliance-risk work is usually not visible to the customer until it is too late (e.g., a security incident that leads to a number of security defects being fixed and security features being added). It is instead pulled internally by the organization; for example, by the Chief Risk Officer and their team.

The final and fourth kind of work is technical debt reduction, which describes the need to perform work on the software and infrastructure codebase that, if not done, will result in the reduced ability to modify or maintain that code in the future. For example, a focus on feature delivery can result in a large accumulation of technical debt. If work is not done to reduce that technical debt, then it could impede future ability to deliver features; for example, by making the software architecture too tangled to innovate on. Table 3.1 summarizes the four flow items.

While the concepts of risk and technical debt are not new in the Flow Framework, the focus on the measurement of each flow item results in a very different set of conclusions as to how they should be managed. In using the Flow Framework, the only technical debt work that should be prioritized is work that increases future flows through the value stream. Tech debt should never be done for the sake of software architecture alone, like using it to improve the separation of architectural layers. This means that the flow of each of the flow items should shape the software architecture and not the other way around, which is counter to the way many enterprise architectures have been evolving.

Flow Items	Delivers	Pulled By	Description	Example artifacts
Features	New business value	Customers	New value added to drive a business result; visible to the customer	Epic, user story, requirement
Defects	Quality	Customers	Fixes for quality problems that affect the customer experience	Bug, problem, incident, change
Risks	Security, governance, compliance	Security and risk officers	Work to address security, privacy, and compliance exposures	Vulnerability, regulatory requirement
Debts	Removal of impediments to future delivery	Architects	Improvement of the software architecture and operational architecture	API addition, refactoring, infrastructure automation

Table 3.1: Flow Items

By focusing first on flow, the other aspects of architecture such as infrastructure cost and information security can be planned for in relation to their business relevance. For instance, investing in architecture to reduce cost before an Incubation Zone product is validated could be a waste when compared to rearchitecting around cost reduction once the product has demonstrated viability and is ready for the Transformation Zone.

The need to focus on flow is similar for products in the Performance Zone. Case in point: At the 2017 DevOps Enterprise Summit, John Allspaw presented a case for treating production software incidents as unplanned investments in a system's architecture.[6] This is precisely the approach that the Flow Framework is intended to measure and support.

Rather than focusing on the software architecture to support any contingency, the focus should be on predicting the future flow of incidents through the product's value stream and on optimizing the architecture for that. This means architecting for resiliency that minimizes the likelihood of those incidents and creating a software architecture, infrastructure architecture, and value stream architecture that can quickly respond to the remaining unforeseen incidents. The result is analogous to what the BMW Group did with the "fingers" structure of the buildings: they predicted how the architecture needs to be adaptable to future flows rather than building in all of the support for those flows up front.

The four flow items follow the MECE principle of being mutually exclusive and collectively exhaustive. In other words, all work that flows in a software value stream is characterized by one—and only one—of the flow items. This means that activities such as prioritization of the various flow items are a zero-sum game, as we will explore in Chapter 4.

Other characterizations of software work items exist, such as Philippe Kruchten and colleagues' decomposition of work into a quadrant of positive/negative and visible/invisible (e.g., features are positive and visible, whereas architecture improvements are positive and invisible).[7] These characterizations can be useful for planning development work. Similarly, ITIL defines the important differences between these problems, incidents, and changes that can be useful for characterizing IT service-desk work.[8] However, these taxonomies are a layer down from the flow items and more useful for characterizing the artifact types being worked on in the delivery of the flow items.

Since the flow items are designed for tracking the most generic characterization of work in a way that is most meaningful to business stakeholders and customers, other taxonomies may crosscut flow items. For example, in SAFe taxonomy, which provides detailed definitions of the many kinds of work items in software delivery, the term for architectural work is *enablers*.[9] This kind of architectural-enabler work can be done to reduce debts, to support the addition of a new feature, to fix a defect, or to address a risk by providing the infrastructure needed to support compliance. This means that architecture work items could fall under any of the flow items. The story is similar for performance improvements, as performance work can be done in support of feature work, such as scaling to a new market, or as part of defect fixes, if the existing user base is experiencing a related set of performance problems.

While the layer below the flow items is critical, the Flow Framework's primary focus is on connecting technology and architecture to the business with the minimal number of concepts that executives and technologists can agree on and understand. As such, each of the units or work items being done by all specialists in the value stream needs to map into one of the four flow items.

Finally, you'll see there is no separate flow item representing improvements to the Value Stream Network to improve flow. In the shift from project to product, the Value Stream Network itself needs to be treated as a product, with its own stable delivery team, and not as a project with a defined end. The majority of Value Stream Network improvements, be they connecting different stakeholders or creating dashboards for flow metrics, will fall on this team. In the cases where teams on a particular value stream need to make changes to their work process—for example, to remove waste by switching from manual compliance checks to an automated security tool—that work falls under the debt flow items for that team.

Conclusion

A large gap exists between what technologists have learned about effective software delivery and how businesses approach software projects. While DevOps and Agile principles have made a significant impact on how technologists work, they have been overly technology centric and have not been adopted broadly by business stakeholders. To bridge the gap, we need a new kind of framework that spans the language of the business with the language of technology and enables the transition from project to product. We need that framework to scale the three ways of DevOps—flow, feedback, and continuous learning—to the entire business. This is the goal of the Flow Framework.

Conclusion to Part I

In Part I, we learned about the five technological revolutions and about how success in the Age of Software is dependent on an organization's ability to shift from project to product. Carlota Perez's work describes how each age is separated into an Installation Period followed by a Turning Point and then a Deployment Period. We are approximately fifty years into the Age of Software and, according to Perez, still somewhere in the midst of the Turning Point.

Organizations that master the software-based means of production and their digital transformations have a chance to both survive and to thrive through this Turning Point. Those that continue to apply managerial paradigms of past ages are likely to decline or die. Tech giants have already mastered this new means of production, and digital startups have been born into this new way of working, but the majority of the world's organizations have not. This is not for want of trying, but the combination of scale, complexity, legacy, and dated managerial paradigms is making that transition impossible to achieve in a time frame that ensures survival. We need a new approach.

Making the transition to thrive in the Age of Software requires a switch from project to product for managing software delivery. Chapter 2 summarized the pitfalls of project-oriented management, while Chapter 3 introduced the Flow Framework as a remedy. The four flow items—features, defects, risks, and debts—provide the simplest and most generic way to unlock the black box of IT and software delivery.

The challenge now is for the business to learn to see what's in that box once opened. Technologists already see it. They are able to track the value delivered on the software products they work on and have had a decade of mastering Agile practices to understand, prioritize, and communicate with each other. The problem is we have not equipped all stakeholders with a common language that bridges the gap between the business and technology. In Part II, the language of Value Stream Metrics is introduced to do just that.

PART II

Flow Framework™

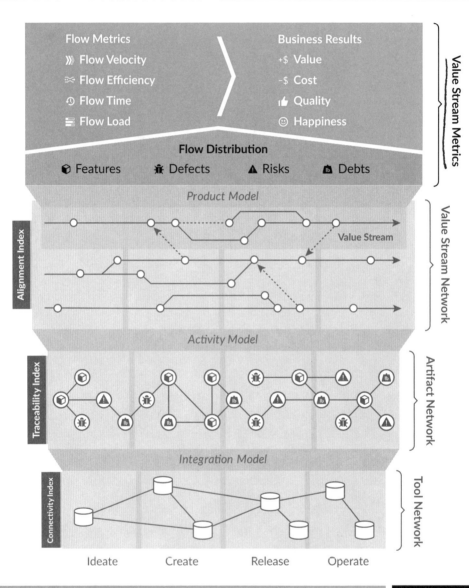

PART II

VALUE STREAM METRICS

In my time at the BMW Group Leipzig plant, I developed a profound appreciation for the direct and explicit relationship between the business and the production line. All of the value streams were visible and clear, and the key metrics, such as lead time and takt time, were universally appreciated and understood. The goal of the Flow Framework is to make software delivery as visible as manufacturing and to do so at the business level. To accomplish that, we need a core set of metrics for tracking the flow of business value in software delivery. In the Flow Framework, those are the Value Stream Metrics.

In Part II, we will define this new set of flow metrics, which provide you with the highest level of visibility of the flow of business value (as defined by the delivery of each of the four flow items). In Part I, we learned about the pitfalls of proxy metrics. In contrast, the goal of flow metrics is to provide a mechanism that correlates the investment in flow for each product's value stream with the business results for that value stream. This provides us with a way of connecting technology investment to business outcomes. And the most important aspect of the Value Stream Metrics portion of the Flow Framework is that we measure flow metrics as well as business results for each product's value stream—be that an external, revenue-generating product; an MVP that is pre-revenue; or a platform component that is only used internally.

Part II will:

- Review how defects have become a key focus of the automotive industry as cars become computers on wheels
- Review how understanding the flow of risks is becoming a board-level concern, as evidenced by the Equifax security breach
- Look at why business leaders need to understand the nature of debts, such as technical and infrastructure debt, by revisiting the downfall of Nokia
- Look at Microsoft's continued success in navigating the Installation Period through the lens of strategic decisions they've made that can be summarized by a business-level understanding of Value Stream Metrics
- Conclude with stories of disruptions through the lens of Value Stream Metrics and a discussion of how visibility into value stream flow may have provided the leadership of these organizations with the knowledge needed to make a better set of decisions

We will examine these stories to learn how to use the Flow Framework to avoid the pitfalls of those who have already fumbled the future in the Age of Software, setting our companies on the successful evolution toward digital innovation.

CHAPTER 4

Capturing Flow Metrics

J ust as the production line provides the BMW Group with visibility into physical production, value streams and the four flow items provide us with the abstraction that we need to see business value flow in software delivery. To obtain that visibility, we first need to identify the key metrics that are most relevant to tracking the productivity of each value stream. We then need a way of applying those metrics to our value streams.

For example, should our goal be to shorten the same lead time across all of our value streams, or do we need a way of deciding which lead time is suitable for each value stream? If we consider what I learned at the BMW Group Leipzig plant, the answer is clearly the latter.

This chapter will continue the plant tour to help paint the picture of how important the tuning of flow metrics is to aligning product-oriented value streams to business goals.

In addition to looking at value stream alignment, we will discuss why the distribution of the four flow items is the critical metric for aligning value streams to business strategy, and how to measure the velocity of the business value that each value stream delivers.

We'll cover how to track flow time and how this measure compares to other time measures used in Lean and Agile. Finally, we'll look at how tracking the load on your value streams can provide you with a high-level leading indicator of the effects of overutilization, which can lead to reduced productivity. The chapter will conclude with an overview of how to measure flow efficiency.

WIP

Architecting for Innovation

After viewing two of the "knuckles" of the 1- and 2-Series production line, Frank turns away from the line and points to a large corridor that connects to the i-Series production line, now nearly in sight. Along this passage, we can see completed i8 models that are flowing into the area where final testing for all the plant's vehicles take place.

"You will notice that this line is very different," Rene says. "It is a much shorter line and has some very interesting new automation."

"The electric model vehicles are innovations from the ground up," Frank says, with visible pride and passion. "Sustainable sourcing, including natural materials from Moses Lake, Washington. The carbon fiber bodies are created here, on site, and the end-to-end process is an industry leader in terms of processing time and environmental footprint. We consider the whole life cycle. Mik, you asked about the windmills outside and how much of the plant's power they generate. Today, they are generating all the power needed to manufacture the electric models. But we are about to start a program where we take the exhausted batteries from the electric models and use them for power storage for the wind turbines."

Every aspect of these cars is designed to optimize end-to-end flow. The idea of reusing the spent batteries in order to help power the plant is yet another expression of the scope of the BMW Group's consideration of continual learning and feedback loops. The feedback loops go far beyond the production line itself, encompassing all points from supply chain to recycling and reuse.

I had seen glimpses of this kind of maturity in IT before—companies that had a deep enough knowledge of the software supply chain to release key software into open source in a way that produced more value for them and the ecosystem than if they had retained the software in house. But effective examples of this kind of maturity are still few and far between. The BMW

Group not only takes a "whole product" approach but a "whole life cycle" approach, reminiscent of what I had learned about the brake software traceability of the Boeing 787 Dreamliner.

Frank and Rene have another innovation to show me. Rene brings my attention to a platform moving a partially assembled car. It looks completely different from the 1- and 2-Series lines that we had seen. The car bodies do not move along a rail. Instead, the car structure is being carried by flat platforms with wheels.

"Those are autonomous platforms," Frank says. "They have replaced the rails on this production line. We can reconfigure the line with software."

With all the autonomous vehicle investment happening across the industry, it seems obvious that the plant would leverage autonomous vehicles for the production line and for the delivery of parts with the plant. But understanding this does not make the concept seem any less magical. I am watching a production line that is capable of reconfiguring itself through software. Perhaps what the BMW Group is doing with physical production is much more related to software delivery pipelines than I expected.

I feel like I am standing on an ever-expanding chasm between the pinnacle of the Deployment Period of the Age of Mass Production and the current state of organizations navigating the Age of Software. It is in this moment I understand why Rene wanted to bring me to the plant. It is not about the i8 or celebrating our recent successes. It is about getting me to understand what he understands.

Having started his career at the Leipzig plant before transitioning to IT, Rene gazes from one age to the other and can see the disconnects. This is very similar to what Carlota Perez shares in her book, having grown up in the Age of Oil and witnessing the transition to the Age of Mass Production.[1] Few people have the kind of perspective that spans two technological revolutions, and those who have it and share it offer invaluable lessons to help guide us through this one.

After reflecting on this and other aspects of the trip to the Leipzig plant, what surprised me most was the level of integration between the business and the production lines. The value streams were a direct mapping of business need to the factory flows. Value was clearly defined by the number of cars and the time it took to deliver each one. There was no complex manual mapping of projects to products to cars and back to the business. The quality of production was simply a count of the cars that needed fixes, as every car that made it down the line would be delivered, even if it required rework of some problematic component. The rework itself was just another part of the flow along the value streams.

That made quality just as visible as velocity. Velocity was the number of cars being completed on the line, and the rework area made quality equally transparent. How could we gain this level of visibility in the four flow items that we were delivering in IT? Perhaps the amorphous nature of software makes gaining visibility of this sort a futile endeavor? But consider that information visualization techniques allow us to "see" information as intangible as stock market trends and the flows of data packets across the internet. There must be a way to apply to IT what the BMW Group applied to manufacturing, and to combine that with the learnings of business intelligence and data visualization.

Notably, at the plant, I saw numerous screens and dashboards showing production information that went beyond what the naked eye could see. The number of car models, variants, and ever-evolving supply chains of parts was highly complex. But it all was tied together in a highly optimized system made visible by the production line and its telemetry. Most important, as the i3 line made clear, the architecture of these value streams and the way they were being visualized was a direct reflection of the needs of the business. Providing us with a similar set of models and abstractions for seeing business value flow through software delivery is the goal of flow metrics.

Understanding Flow Distribution

The underlying flow metric (Figure 4.1) is the simplest but also the most consequential. We need to track the target *flow distribution* of each of

Distribution = guardrails for each flow items

the four flow items for each value stream. For example, a value stream for a new product is likely to require a large proportion of features that need to be delivered in time for launch. In this case, a majority of the total work can be committed to feature flow; in other words, the value stream will be optimized for the delivery of new business value. Assuming that the new product has a limited number of customers prior to launch, such as beta testers, the amount of defect flow is likely to be low. If the new product is an experiment that is not intended to be released publicly, then the ratio of work on risks will likely be low as well. However, if the product is intended to be released to the market, the amount of risk work can be higher; and more contingencies for missed defects should be allocated.

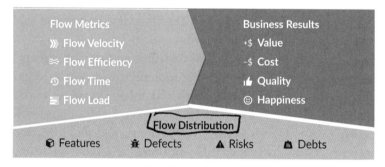

Figure 4.1: Flow Metrics

In contrast, consider a value stream for an existing and entrenched product, such as a legacy back-end service that will continue to exist only to support mobile applications with data. The flow distribution for the value stream could be set to optimize for risk reduction and defect fixes, with minimal or no investment in feature flow.

Flow Distribution: *The proportion of each flow item within a value stream, adjusted depending on the needs of each stream to maximize business value.*

We can use flow distribution to tailor value streams to the type of results that we need to deliver to the business. In addition, flow distribution can be tuned to the particular product-maturity life cycle stage, or zone, that the product is in. For instance, I have deployed both the Three Horizons Framework methodology[2] and, more recently, Moore's Zone Management at Tasktop. Making this explicit to each of the managers and teams working on the corresponding products allowed them to set the flow distribution and the talent and processes supporting the value streams, matching the business goals of the horizon or zone.

In the end, it is the teams on the value stream that will know best how to match flow distribution for business results (e.g., taking down some technical debt at the start of a release cycle to accelerate feature flow toward the end of it). But both the teams and the leadership need to have a shared understanding of the flow distribution for which a particular value stream is optimized.

In addition to defining the flow distribution for value streams and investment zones, it can be set directionally for an entire organization in order to align all delivery with a high-level business goal. Later in this chapter, we will examine how Bill Gates set a high-level goal of focusing on risk and security improvements through Microsoft's Trustworthy Computing initiative, and how he later focused on feature flow in order to play disruption defense with pivoting Microsoft's products to the web.

Flow distribution has far-reaching implications for how a product's value stream is structured and managed. A legacy product that is a candidate for end-of-life or divestiture demonstrates this, as it should see no debt investment. If the organization is going through a replatforming, including an end-of-life value stream in this replatforming would most likely be a waste of time and resources. In contrast, if an organization is under threat from nimbler digital natives, it could be critical to throw away an old platform and invest in a cloud-native architecture. This part of the organization's value stream network can then be optimized to rapidly bring new features to market and hypothesis testing with customer feedback and usage data.

In addition to tuning flow distribution to the type of investment that represents success for a particular value stream, flow distribution is also the primary metric for evolving and refining that investment over time.

In this scenario, a new product's value stream was tuned to maximizing the flow of features. Once that product was made generally available, the flow distribution could be used to predict capacity constraints going forward. For example, seasoned product and engineering managers know the need to build in additional capacity for dealing with the number of support tickets and incidents that can arise in the release cycle post-launch, and then for reducing technical debt that was accrued in the release cycle that followed. However, all too often, the business does not have a vocabulary or model for understanding these critical shifts in flow distribution over time.

What can result in this scenario is a business that expects the rate of feature flow to continue post release, which means that insufficient capacity is going to supporting the new users or to ensuring that the next set of features can be implemented at reasonable cost by reducing the technical debts incurred in creating the latest set of features. This is exactly the scenario that we see playing out in Figure 4.2, which shows the flow distribution data for the twelve months following the 1.0 release of a product that I was involved with called Tasktop Hub.

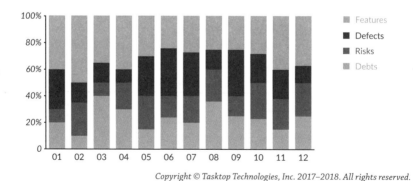

Figure 4.2: Dashboard Showing Flow Distribution

Flow Distribution

What we can see from the flow distribution in the Hub value stream is a pattern that experienced product managers have learned to expect following a new product introduction: The ramp-up to the initial release required tremendous focus on the completion of features. There was a race against time, as the company's success depended on whether enough features could be delivered in time for launch. And the entire business hinged on the success of this release, similar to how Boeing's business hinged on the introduction of a new plane. This was a story I repeatedly told to the product and engineering teams involved, and I met with the product and engineering leadership for that value stream every two weeks in order to track feature progress.

The organization was already aligned to value streams, so additional funding was made available mid-budget cycle in order to accelerate the velocity of feature delivery. While our Agile and DevOps practices meant that adding staff did increase capacity, we were still up against a hard limitation of a six-month-maximum ramp time for a new engineer for this product due to the complexity of the problem domain and the codebase.

I allocated additional budget to the value stream, but with nine months to the release date, it was clear that throwing more people at the problem would have limited returns, per Fred Brooks's *The Mythical Man-Month: Essays on Software Engineering*.[3]

With a product mind-set, investing new staff in a value stream needs to be modeled in a similar way to how ramp time for salespeople needs to be understood for a functional sales model. Any investment that has to produce results within six months has to come from existing—not new—capacity.

The teams suggested that additional technical debt could be taken on in order to allocate more flow to delivering features instead of reducing debts. On the Hub value stream, our target debt work for each release was 20% of flow distribution, a number that we based on our own historical flow metrics as well as, and similar to, best practices reported by others. The teams working on the release knew the trade-off well, as did I, and made it clear to the other managers that not paying down this debt each sprint would significantly reduce our feature capacity post release. I knew that time to market was more critical here than feature velocity post release, and we collectively decided that this was the best path.

A critical factor in that decision was that Tasktop's Fortune 500 customer base had taken multiple months to deploy new releases in the past. We had a historical sense for the post release flow distribution of those releases, and with that information, we were comfortable accepting this impact on the future feature flow. But we did not predict the impact on this value stream that was to come.

It turned out that customers adopted the product much more quickly than we had anticipated. As we were nearing the public release date, we learned after the fact that a major telecom provider that was in the beta program was using a beta release in large-scale production. As Figure 4.3 depicts, the sprints following the release had much more allocation to defects than we had predicted. There were more key features on the backlog that needed to get done, even with that reduced capacity.

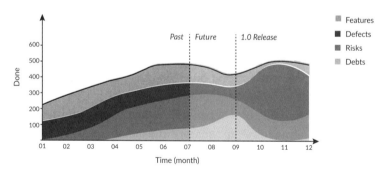

Figure 4.3: Flow Distribution Timeline

So again, the work on debts was sidelined and went to an all-time low for this team due to all the urgent feature work and unplanned extra defect work. Technical debt tends to compound from release to release, and as the figure depicts, the team had to start paying the piper as feature delivery started trending to zero, which is unsustainable for a product that requires ongoing innovation.

In hindsight, the seasoned product manager responsible for the release had predicted the likelihood of this happening and communicated it to the management team. But at a leadership level, we had not adjusted the customer and partner redeployment plans accordingly until after this trend was clear (while doing a quarterly planning session with this flow distribution dashboard in hand). It was the business-level understanding of the current and predicted future flow distribution that allowed us to adjust all the business initiatives accordingly. More importantly, we learned that at a business level, we needed to make flow distribution predictions much more visible across all departments and teams who were dependent on future delivery.

What flow distribution gives us is a zero-sum mechanism for deciding how one or more value streams should support business priorities. If we think back to the Leipzig plant, everything in the lines is architected around the kind of flow required of the lines. This is why the structure of the i8- and i3-model lines and the 1- and 2-Series lines is so dramatically different. Even though the cars made on those production lines look roughly the same size and shape, the production lines are tuned to very different business needs and constraints, with one directed more toward innovation and the other toward high volume.

This is how we need to treat our software value streams. Flow distribution gives us a mechanism for evolving those value streams to the businesses' evolving needs over time. However, unlike physical production, we are not going to set up separate and isolated lines of production for our software value streams.

As we will see later in this chapter, a single Value Stream Network can support tuning and managing flow distribution across product lines and over time. Everything within those value streams can then be tuned by the teams to produce the best flow distribution to meet the current business needs, as we saw the BMW Group do. This tuning is inclusive of everything, from the kind of talent working on a particular value stream to a value stream flow–centric way of thinking about software architecture.

Flow Metric	Description	Example
Flow Distribution	Mutually Exclusive and Comprehensively Exhaustive (MECE) allocation of flow items in a particular flow state across a measure of time.	Proportion of each flow unit actively being worked on in a particular sprint.
Flow Velocity	Number of flow items done in a given time.	Debts resolved for a particular release.
Flow Time	Time elapsed from when a flow item enters the value stream (flow state = active) to when it is released to the customer (flow state = done).	Time it takes to deliver a new feature to a customer from when the feature is accepted.
Flow Load	Number of flow items with flow state as active or waiting, (i.e., work in progress [WIP]).	Flow load that exceeds a certain threshold adversely impacts flow velocity.
Flow Efficiency	The proportion of time flow items are actively worked on to the total time elapsed.	Flow efficiency decreases when dependencies cause teams to wait on others.

Table 4.1: Flow Metrics

The power of flow distribution is that it allows the business to do explicitly and at scale the kind of planning that product and engineering teams and managers already do as part of their daily work. Thinking in terms of flow distribution trade-offs elevates the understanding of software-delivery trade-offs to the business. This kind of thinking is second nature for business leaders that have been software engineers, such as the CEOs of the tech giants. The goal of the Flow Framework is to make this kind of decision making accessible to the entire business, not just those with a background in coding and software product management.

The zero-sum game of flow-distribution trade-offs forces the business to make the kinds of trade-offs that the development team lead has to make constantly as unplanned work enters the value stream. If too many defects come in, features will be pushed out. If pressure from the business to deliver new features while fixing defects does not abate for several quarters, debt backlogs could get to the point where new-feature delivery will no longer be feasible. If risks are not explicitly prioritized on the team's backlog, they will never get implemented, as they tend not to be visible to the customer or the business. Delivery teams innately know this, but when the business stakeholders do not, we should not be surprised that decision making seems uninformed and flawed.

To see a balanced flow distribution, flow items should be of a similar level of effort or size. If the average feature takes four times the work of the average defect, a stacked bar chart would show four times the defect compared to feature flow. This is not inherently bad, as the point of flow items is that they encapsulate units of value and work that are meaningful to the business, however that value is assigned. In practice, these kinds of skews can be misleading to business stakeholders. As a result, at Tasktop, we have chosen to set flow item counts by like-sized work items in our Agile model. For example, feature flow items are mapped to user stories, as those are of similar size to defects rather than to "epics," which are much longer lived (see the Integration Model in Chapter 9).

Flow Velocity

Flow distribution can span any time frame or state-of-flow items, be that understanding everything active or done for the current release or estimating future capacity. In addition to distribution, we need a more specific measure of how much business value is being delivered to the customer. To do that, we need to measure the number of each flow item being completed over a unit of time.

This is *flow velocity*. It is adapted from the Agile concept of velocity, which determines how many units of work (e.g., story points) a team delivers in a time period (e.g., a two-week sprint).[4] Flow velocity uses the same concept but applies it to the four flow items and is a simpler and less granular measure. For instance, if ten features and five risks are completed for a release, the flow velocity for that release is fifteen. Figure 4.4 shows a sample flow velocity dashboard that visualizes progress toward meeting a value stream's flow velocity target for each flow item, contrasting progress to the last iteration's total.

A key difference of flow velocity is that it is a simpler measure than Agile velocity, as it does not rely on estimation of the size or scope of work or the priority of each flow item. That kind of decomposition can still happen at the Agile development level. In SAFe terminology, a feature can be connected into an epic and composed of a number of user stories, each of which has a story point estimate.[5] That level of decomposition can be critical to a disciplined prioritization of work.

The Flow Framework assumes that prioritization is being done within each of the flow items, just as it assumes that business value definition is being done; and it only focuses on the end-to-end flow of the corresponding units. As long as each type of artifact, also known as work item in the Agile model, is mapped to one of the flow items, both the flow distribution and flow velocity will be representative of all of the work being delivered.

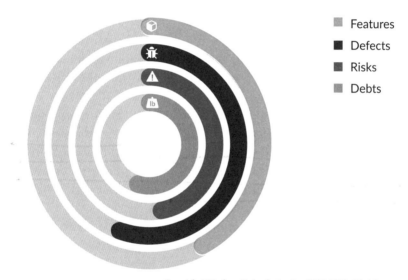

Features
Defects
Risks
Debts

Figure 4.4: Sample Flow Velocity Dashboard

With the combination of flow items and flow velocity, we are able to measure how much of each flow item was delivered and plan ahead for what is required to attain the desired future state needed to meet business goals. For example, if the flow velocity on features is too low for a particular value stream to meet business goals, we can start asking questions about what could increase it, be that investments in talent, architecture, or infrastructure.

In the Flow Framework, flow velocity is the empirical measure of productivity based on direct observation of value streams. It supersedes proxies for productivity, such as lines of code written, function points added, deploys per day, or the time it takes to go from code commit to code deploy. Those proxy metrics can be critical to understanding different parts of a value stream. For example, in *Accelerate* by Nicole Forsgren, Jez Humble, and Gene Kim, the *State of DevOps* survey results indicate that deploys per day correlate with both IT and organizational performance.[6] This implies that deployment automation is a common bottleneck for IT organizations that are still growing their DevOps practices. But at organizations like Tasktop, which has deployed continuous integration, "commit to deploy" time and "deploys per day" are not limiting factors of the value delivered to customers. Their measurement, along with other metrics like lines of code per product, are still informative and useful for spotting anomalies, but they are not a primary or business-level metric.

Like many other organizations born around the Turning Point of the Age of Software, we realized years ago that we needed a metric that represented productivity from our customers' point of view, in terms of how much we delivered to customers and how quickly we went from accepting the customer request to delivery. This is where flow velocity and flow time come in.

Measurements such as the number of lines of code determine how much of a particular type of work was done by a developer, not how many units of value were delivered. A single feature, such as changing the behavior of the "Like" button in a product, could take very few lines of code but a large amount of analysis and design. A single line change in a mission-critical mainframe application can take days of impact analysis. So, while code-centric metrics are relevant to understanding more fine-grained aspects of work happening on various value streams, they are not suitable for encapsulating business value.

Flow items are explicitly tied to business value. For instance, it is the role of a business analyst or product manager to define whether a particular feature has value to the customer based on the needs and pull of the customer. The same goes for defects, risks, and debts. Before any flow item enters the value stream, it should have its business value explicitly defined. Notably, the Flow Framework does not provide guidance on how to define that value (e.g., how to design a feature that drives adoption or how to determine which risks should be prioritized for resolution ahead of others). That is the role of Agile frameworks and product management processes. The Flow Framework hinges on that value being defined and measures the flow of value to the customer so that those defining the value can establish a fast feedback loop with their customers and the market.

Flow items can vary significantly in size, which may make it tempting to give them "story point" or "T-shirt" sizing.[7] In Agile frameworks, these measures, as well as business-value rankings, are critical to prioritizing and planning what work should be done and when. However, the Flow Framework is targeted not at prioritizing work but at making that flow of work and its results visible. In addition, story-point or T-shirt sizing is targeted at large-scale software delivery, where the numbers of the flow items are large. As such, the law of large numbers applies (which states that the likelihood of an occurrence evens out given enough trials or instances),[8] and we can rely on the amount of work required to complete a particular flow item to fall on a common distribution when measured in aggregate. In other words, with a sufficiently large number of flow items, the scenario where all flow items in one time period are large and those in another are all small should be rare.

Given that the flow velocity is measured empirically by inspecting the Value Stream Network, we can also determine if there are meaningful size differences across flow items. One value stream may be defining features in a very coarse way while another creates very fine-grained features. Or we may discover that a legacy mainframe value stream delivers very large amounts of business value with a very small number of features delivered. In addition, product managers will also define features in ways that are particular to the technology, market, and customer for the value stream that they are supporting. As such, flow velocity metrics are more suited to track productivity and delivery trends *within* a value stream than *across* value streams. However, when the context of a flow item is similar—for example, the need to implement a regulatory requirement such as from GDPR (General

Data Protection Regulation) across all products—cross-value-stream comparisons can become relevant. If one value stream is much more productive at implementing a new privacy protocol than others, there could be a case for extracting the code that it is using into a common API that will be used by other value streams for the same purpose. This is exactly how developers think already, and this kind of value stream thinking can make the case for investing in an API as a new value stream easier to justify for the organization.

Flow Time

Flow distribution and flow velocity provide an empirical measure of how much of which kind of work is done over a period of time, but they do not indicate how quickly that work cycles through the system. In order to determine the speed at which we are delivering (e.g., to understand time to market for a particular feature or across a set of features), we need to measure flow time.

In Lean manufacturing, two key metrics are used for process improvement: lead time and cycle time. Lead time focuses on measuring time through an entire process, while cycle time focuses on the time it takes to complete a step within the process. From the last Deployment Period of the Age of Mass Production, we know that both of these metrics are key to improving production processes. Cycle time can help identify constraints—where the step with the longest cycle time will typically be the bottleneck—while lead time tells us the time it takes for the end-to-end process to run (for example, starting at the customer order for the car and ending with delivery). Lead time is cited as the best predictor of performance in manufacturing.[9] The goal of the Flow Framework is to provide an equally meaningful end-to-end measure of the time it takes to deliver value via software.

The challenge with both lead time and cycle time is that their use in Agile and DevOps literature has been ambiguous and has too often deviated from the original meaning. "Code commit to deploy lead time" is a common metric used by the DevOps community, for instance. However, if you take a customer-centric and value stream–centric point of view (versus a developer-centric one), it is not a measure of lead time but a measure of development cycle time.

While it is feasible to create different subsets of lead time, to avoid confusion, the Flow Framework uses the Lean metric of flow time (Figure 4.5), as proposed by Dominica DeGrandis in her book *Making Work Visible: Exposing Time Theft to Optimize Work & Flow.*[10] Flow time starts when a flow item is accepted into the value stream (e.g., when a feature is scheduled for a release, or when a customer ticket is reported and the corresponding defect starts being investigated for resolution). Since it is a customer-centric measure, flow time is measured in "wall clock" time; in other words, as soon as the work starts, so does the clock. And it does not stop during off hours and weekends but runs until the flow item has been deployed to a customer.

Flow time is based on the transitions that flow items make across four different flow states. The four flow states are new, waiting, active, and done. These states are based on a generalized version of all of the workflow states supported by the fifty-five different Agile, DevOps, and issue-tracking tools used by the 308 organizations we studied at Tasktop.

For example, lead time for a single flow item is measured by comparing the time from when the item starts in the "new" state to when the item enters the "done" state. Similarly, mean time to repair (MTTR) is measured by comparing the time from "new" to "done" for a defect corresponding to the outage, which may have started its life cycle as an incident. Flow time is measured by comparing the time from "active" to "done." These flow states follow the MECE (mutually exclusive and comprehensively exhaustive) principle, and as a result, all of the finer-grained workflow states in the tools studied can be mapped into one of the four flow states.

In the study, we encountered organizations with over 200 different workflow states on a single artifact type, such as a requirement. Regardless of how many states exist, the Activity Model (Chapter 9) is used to map the more generic flow states in order to provide consistent visibility of flow time across value streams. The comparison of lead time, flow time, and cycle time, as well as the corresponding flow-item states, are visible in Figure 4.5.

Figure 4.5: Comparison of Lead Time, Flow Time, and Cycle Time

Flow time is a primary metric in the Flow Framework because it gives us a comprehensive measurement of how long it takes to deliver a flow item, from the decision to take on the work to the value being delivered to the customer. Across value streams, measures of lead time remain important (e.g., to track the longer period of time from when a customer requests a feature). But they are outside of the scope of the Flow Framework, as they typically involve numerous other organizational processes, especially when there are many more customer requests than can be taken on in a value stream. For example, popular open-source projects I have worked on have had a hundred times more feature requests than capacity for any given release. While these projects had abysmal lead time, their success was a function of flow time, as that's what determined how many planned features they were delivering.

Flow Time: *The duration that it takes for a flow item to go from being accepted for work into the value stream to completion, including both active and wait time.*

While separating flow time from lead time is important for products with large backlogs of customer requests, for products with smaller backlogs, the two metrics will be more closely converged. As such, lead time will continue to provide meaningful measure, as summarized by Carmen DeArdo in his approach to deploying lead-time metrics along with Flow Framework concepts at Nationwide Insurance.[11]

Within a value stream, cycle time becomes very important; for example, to determine if there is a bottleneck in a particular stage of the value stream, such as user-experience design (UX) or quality assurance (QA). But when measuring the end-to-end value stream, the most important metric is flow time. Business needs for flow velocity and flow time should drive the architecture of a value stream, exactly as we saw at the Leipzig plant. If the Value Stream Network needs to support a four-week flow time for features, it is unlikely that will be achieved with large batch sizes and a development cycle time longer than two weeks. Flow times that are longer than desired provide an anchor for what to investigate within a value stream to drive improvement. (The contributors to longer-than-desired flow time are summarized in Part III.)

Flow time in software delivery works differently than it does in manufacturing because a flow item does not need to take a linear path through a value stream (as we will review further in Part III). Certain flow items can be "fast tracked" through a value stream, bypassing large numbers of stages, which is not feasible in a production line. For example, a high-severity incident identified by a monitoring tool or support team may be the result of a software defect; and the service-level agreement (SLA) for that particular value stream might specify a required flow time of under twenty-four hours for high-severity fixes. To support such a flow, the Value Stream Network's Activity Model (Chapter 9) can specify a process where that defect lands immediately on a development-team backlog for the current sprint, without requiring upstream phases such as design, planning, and prioritization. Similarly, an incubation product with no external releases could skip downstream stages, such as regulatory certification. This means that different kinds of flow items can exhibit very different flow times, depending on which parts of the Value Stream Network they flow through.

While tuning these various flows is critical to creating a responsive software-delivery organization and an effective value stream model, it is the flow time measurements that will ensure that all the cycle times of the various stages are optimized as well. For example, defects originating from high-severity production incidents might need a target flow time of hours. A feature flow time of four weeks may be adequate for a mature product, whereas one week may be required for an experimental incubation-zone product that needs a faster cadence of hypothesis testing.

Flow time is the most meaningful metric to tune to business results, as it starts when the flow item has been explicitly accepted (e.g., a new feature) or implicitly accepted (e.g., an automatically escalated incident) for delivery. Failing to set and manage the various flow time targets that meet business needs can create an organization that is highly responsive to defects and incidents but is left wondering why it takes so long to deliver new value to a customer through features. This is another potential pitfall of local optimization of the value stream.

Flow Load

The goal of *flow load* is to provide a leading indicator of any problems that will affect flow velocity and flow time. Flow load is the measure of all the active flow items that are in progress within a given value stream. It is a measure of how much concurrent demand there is in the value stream and its work-in-progress (WIP) measure, common in manufacturing and proposed by DeGrandis for managing flow in software delivery. As DeGrandis details, excess WIP is the enemy of productivity due to the negative effects that overutilization has on output.[12]

Flow load is the total number of flow items being worked on, (e.g., in an "active" or "waiting" state) within a particular value stream. If you imagine a value stream as a pipe, where all flow items that have not been started or those that have been completed are outside the two ends of the pipe, the flow load is the number of units inside the pipe. Flow load is the load on the pipe, inclusive of all the partially completed work.

> **Flow Load:** The number of flow items being actively worked on in a value stream, denoting the amount of WIP (work in progress).

Excessive flow load can be correlated to inefficiency. For example, Reinertsen states that excess utilization of a value stream dramatically affects velocity due to excess queue times.[13] As with the other flow metrics, the Flow Framework does not provide absolute numbers to specify what the flow load should be for a particular value stream. By ensuring that flow load is tracked, the Flow Framework enables the correlation of increased flow load to changes in flow velocity and flow time. The goal is to provide the business with a leading indicator of the point at which taking on too many flow items in parallel reduces output.

As Reinertsen points out, the tendency for the business is to maximize utilization of the resources in the value stream.[14] In manufacturing, this could suggest ensuring that each robot is 100% utilized. Goldratt demonstrates how flawed this approach is for manufacturing,[15] while Reinertsen provides proof of the negative effects of over-utilization for product development.[16] The corresponding practice in software delivery is the tendency to set the delivery of flow items such as features to 100% allocation for the teams building the software. As DeGrandis summarizes, the result of seeking full utilization is similarly problematic for software delivery as it is for manufacturing, having a negative effect on flow velocity and flow time.[17]

The flow-load metric, when correlated to the other flow metrics, makes the result clear and provides visibility to setting flow load to a level that maximizes flow velocity and minimizes flow time. Note that this level may vary by value stream. For example, a mature software product for a well-defined market with a seasoned set of teams may be able to take on a higher flow load than a smaller team with an exploratory product, which requires iterating on MVPs and taking on large amounts of unplanned work as the new product goes through customer development.

Flow Efficiency

Building on this approach to tracking flow time, we can also track the time that each flow item is being actively worked on. This provides us with the final metric of flow efficiency, as depicted in Figure 4.6. The purpose of tracking flow efficiency is to determine the proportion of time that flow items are actively worked on compared to the total time spent in the value stream. The lower the flow efficiency, the more waste can be attributed to flow items stagnating in a waiting state. The more items that are waiting, the more work in progress (WIP) and the larger the queues in the value stream. As queues grow, overutilization and context switching lead to more waste, and the delays compound.

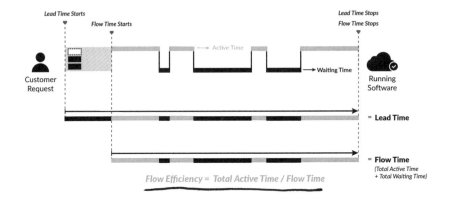

Figure 4.6: Flow Efficiency

While it is reasonable to expect some wait states and queuing of flow items, the purpose of tracking flow efficiency is to identify value streams with excessive wait times that lead to increases in flow time or reduced flow velocity. Excessive dependencies within a value stream, such as the development team waiting for test data sets, are made visible through a reduction in flow efficiency. Since flow efficiency is based on flow time and not cycle time, it captures wait times both upstream and downstream of development. If the development team is waiting on user interface design while the designers are allocated to other work, flow efficiency will drop due to the corresponding features being in a wait state, as neither team is working on them. As such, value-stream bottlenecks can be identified by tracking down the causes of the reduction in flow efficiency.

Conclusion

What this chapter has shown is that we need to make our software products and value streams just as visible as they are in a production line. Due to the amorphous nature of our products, this may seem more challenging to do in software than it is for manufacturing. However, we have no lack of data collection and information visualization approaches at our disposal. The Leipzig plant itself has countless screens and digital dashboards to make visible the telemetry and reports of production that cannot be seen with the naked eye. The problem is not with visualizing the information; the problem is that, at a business level, we have not come up with a compelling set of abstractions for what to visualize.

Contrast this with the DevOps team, who knows the exact telemetry to show, such as deploys per day and change success rate. Or contrast it with the development team, who uses Scrum or kanban boards to make work in progress visible to the entire team. In other words, the work should already be visible at the specialist and team level. It's the business-level visibility that organizations lack. This is what flow metrics provide.

Measuring the four flow metrics in real time across all value streams may seem difficult, due to the complexity of modern toolchains and delivery pipelines. Answers to this difficulty will be outlined in Part III, where we will explore how a Value Stream Network needs to be created and connected to support both this kind of flow and feedback. But before we do that, we need to define the business results that are the goal of tracking flow in the first place.

CHAPTER 5

Connecting to Business Results

(handwritten margin note:)
1 Value
2 Cost
3 Quality
4 happiness (staff)

The last chapter reviewed how we can measure the First Way of DevOps, end-to-end flow, by using flow metrics. This chapter explores the Second Way of DevOps: feedback. Feedback gives us the capability of connecting software-production results back to the business. What we need next is to establish a set of outcome-based metrics that support a business-level view of the Second Way. By establishing such metrics, we create a feedback loop between flow metrics and the business outcomes that they generate, which then creates the continual learning and experimentation loops that enable high-performance IT organizations to thrive.

Product management uses well established criteria for tracking the phases, processes, resources, and dependencies needed to get to successful project conclusion. In contrast, the key aspect of tracking business outcomes using the Flow Framework is that they are tracked continually for each product-oriented value stream. This is in contrast to many existing approaches, which track metrics according to project or organizational structures. It is this shift in what we measure that is key to accomplishing the move from project to product, as accurate feedback at the right level of granularity is essential to supporting decision making.

In this chapter, we will cover how to measure both value and cost for each product's value stream. We will then discuss measurement of product quality from a value stream and customer-oriented perspective. The last business outcome metric we will address is the happiness of the staff contributing to the value stream. Finally, we'll review the key measures to track in value stream dashboards.

BMW TRIP Tuning Production to Business Outcomes

"We could not predict precisely how quickly the electric-car market would evolve," Frank says, "so we did not want to create the kind of automation that you see with the 1- and 2-Series. We wanted to create something much more instead—what you call Agile—so that we could scale and adapt as needed. We have a much tighter feedback loop here in order to be able to respond to the shifts in electric-car market demand. For example, Norway just announced a plan that by 2025, all cars sold should be zero emissions.[1] We are able to evolve the line to scale up production if we see such increases in demand. So, we created this line with a different set of trade-offs. The takt time of an i3 is eight minutes, which is much different than the 1- and 2-Series lines you just saw, where work at each station needs to be completed in the takt time of seventy seconds. Each line is tailored to meet different goals of our business and of our customers."

This epitomized value stream thinking to me. When market and business demands change, more can be invested into a particular product. The architecture of the value stream itself can be extended. Most important of all, the BMW Group has built these lines with that adaptability in mind. Some months after the trip, I learned that the plant did indeed increase i3 and i8 production from 130 to 200 units per day.[2]

It strikes me that this is exactly how we need to think about software delivery. Instead of pretending that we can precisely predict the future in terms of product market fit and scalability, we need to clearly define the success metrics for our value streams and create them in a way that supports adaptability and extensibility. We need to architect our software and our organizations around our value streams, not the other way around.

"So, is this what the i8 line looks like?" I ask, as I cannot help but wonder about the intricacy and automation of the i8 line;

to me, the i8 is one of the most impressive vehicles to be mass produced.

"No, no," says Frank. "The i8 line is by far the shortest line in the building, a fraction of the i3 line, which itself is a fraction of the 1- and 2-Series lines. Guess what the takt time of the i8 is."

"Eight minutes, like the i3?"

"Very wrong." Frank says. "It is thirty minutes—you will see why shortly. But first, let's take a look how the i3s are built."

Connecting Flow Metrics to Business Results

The BMW Group cars' takt times were attuned to the different business needs of each car, as were the target results for each car. Similarly, business targets will vary across your value streams. A key goal of the Flow Framework is to provide you with a core set of metrics to measure each of your value streams. While a much broader set of metrics specific to your business is likely to be needed, the Flow Framework requires that you have metrics for each product's value, cost, quality, and happiness (see Figure 5.1 and Table 5.1).

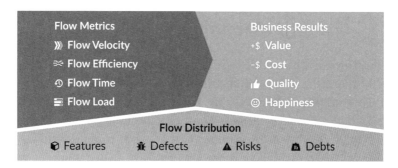

Figure 5.1: Connecting Flow Metrics to Business Results

How you measure these will be particular to your organization, and different organizations will have different approaches to measuring each of these outcomes. However, for the correlation of software delivery to business outcomes, each of these measurements needs to be tracked for each value stream. In Part III, we will review any changes that you must make to your tool network to enable this kind of metrics collection, such as instrumenting employee surveys with a value stream indicator to ensure that the happiness metric can be correlated to the corresponding value stream.

Business Result	Measures	Examples
Value	Benefit to the business produced by the value stream.	Revenue, monthly recurring revenue, annual contract value, monthly active users.
Cost	Cost of the value stream to the business.	Cost of all staff, operations, and infrastructure supporting the value stream. FFEs assigned to the value stream.
Quality	Quality of the product produced by the value stream as perceived by a customer.	Escaped defects, tickets filed, renewal rate, expansion rate, Net Promoter Score (NPS).
Happiness	Engagement of the staff working on the value stream.	Employee Net Promoter Score (eNPS), employee engagement.

Table 5.1: Business Results Metrics

① Measuring Value

The most important metric for each value stream is an objective measure of value. This should come directly from the financial metrics used by the organization. For example, for a customer-facing product, the metric could be overall revenue from that product or monthly recurring revenue. The measure of value can be more complex and include different types of revenue or renewal rates. Multi-sided markets, where users and buyers are separate, may require a special treatment of value (e.g., in ad-supported business models, where a value stream delivers features to users but revenue comes via banner ads). In this case, a proxy for revenue can be used, such as monthly active users, which can then be related to revenue. The same can be done for pre-revenue value streams, as long as you use a metric that translates to revenue once the product and value stream scales. Additional leading indicators for revenue can also be put into the value bucket, like sales-pipeline growth or customer satisfaction (e.g., NPS) generated by the value stream.

An important aspect of measuring revenue per value stream are the systems for tracking revenue, such as accounting and customer relationship management (CRM). These systems need to be set up in a way to connect revenue results back to a single product's value stream; and this can become problematic if suites of products are sold without tracking purchasing and use of the SKUs within those products.

Some product value streams may not be monetized directly: for example, a value stream for a software platform component that is used by internal developers, or an internal application like a billing or transaction-processing system. In this case, these value streams will not have a direct revenue metric but will still need to have value outcome metrics defined. Those metrics can be the indirect value that's generated by the product.

As we will see in Part III, the dependencies between value streams that show up in the Value Stream Network will make the revenue-generating value streams that they support explicit and visible. If a platform or SDK component supports ten value streams, all or a portion of the value generated by those value streams can be used. Alternatively, internal value metrics can be used, such as the adoption rate of an internal product. For example, if an internal billing system was once used by a dozen revenue-generating value streams but eleven of those value streams now use a cloud-based billing provider instead, the lack of revenue support by the internal billing system's value stream can be used to make the case of end-of-life for that system.

This kind of decision making is key to a product-oriented mind-set, and the measurement of the business results is critical to understanding the trade-offs. (Additional guidance on setting up your Value Stream Network to easily track these metrics is in Part III.)

②Value Stream Cost

Value stream cost includes all costs associated with delivery for a particular product. This is similar to considering the total cost of ownership for everything involved with delivery for that value stream, and it is analogous to the practices of "costing by value stream" in manufacturing.[3] However, it only includes the delivery costs, not shared costs like marketing and sales, which, for most organizations, will be difficult or impossible to attempt to map to a single value stream.

When we consider costing by value stream, project-oriented management costing models and approaches to resource allocation break down. If a staff member can be assigned to more than one value stream, deriving a reliable allocation of their time to that value stream will be error prone at best. One Fortune 100 IT organization that I worked with measured how many projects each developer was allocated to and found the number to be between six and twelve per year.

The inability to account costs per value stream is another example of why a project-oriented approach breaks down in scaling software delivery. If you cannot accurately measure costs per value stream, you cannot reliably determine product profitability or other business goals that are key to software innovation. This is not to say that there will not be shared resources used by a value stream (e.g., a graphic designer who supports multiple products), but these resources should be the exception, not the norm.

Value stream cost needs to account for all direct costs as well as the proportion of shared service costs used by the value stream. This can include staff costs (internal and contractors), license costs, and infrastructure costs (internal or hosted). The key variable is that each dedicated service is assigned to the value stream that uses it, and each shared resource is assigned proportionally to its usage by that value stream. If a cloud-hosting platform is used, compute- and data-service billing must be allocated to each value stream to get a complete picture of costs.

The combination of measuring both value and cost enables the implementation of measuring life cycle profit for each value stream. In *The Principles of Product Development Flow: Second Generation Lean Product Development*, Donald G. Reinertsen made the case for life cycle profit as the primary and, by far, most meaningful metric for product delivery.[4] However, keeping these two metrics separated also allows us to measure outcomes for pre-revenue value streams as well as internal ones.

③ Value Stream Quality

There is a vast amount of literature on software quality metrics. In addition, the DevOps Research and Assessment (DORA) *2017 State of DevOps Report* identified a correlation between quality metrics, such as escaped defects with IT and organizational performance.[5] Due to the focus of value streams on the customer, these kinds of customer-visible metrics should be used for the quality bucket. In addition to escaped defects, the number of incidents, ticket counts, and other customer-success metrics can populate this bucket. Quality metrics that are not visible to the customer, like defect aging and change success rate, can provide important leading indicators of quality problems. However, they should remain one level down, as the Flow Framework focuses on customer- and business-visible metrics.

The key is to track the quality metrics separately for each value stream to make quality trade-offs visible. For instance, if a push for time to market comes at the cost of quality, this should be visible in the resulting quality metrics, as those may be a leading indicator for upcoming revenue or renewal losses and the need to allocate additional future flow distribution on defects to remedy the situation.

④ Value Stream Happiness

The final metric tracks the health of the value stream. In software delivery, value-adding activities are done by people undertaking tasks, such as business analysis, design, architecture, coding, test automation, site-reliability engineering, and support. It is now possible to automate most of the manual processes in software delivery, such as manual testing. The result is that the productivity of the value stream is determined by value-creating activities, like designing screens or writing automated tests. Even as automation increases (e.g., via future AI tools that automatically generate tests), tech companies have long realized that the limiting factor to productivity is the creative work being done by teams.

Daniel Pink and others have demonstrated that happy and engaged staff produce better results when creative work is involved.

Project-oriented management gets in the way of the autonomy, mastery, and purpose identified by Pink as key to job satisfaction, whereas product-oriented stability of work and teams promotes them.[6]

In addition to the need to measure and improve individual and team happiness and productivity, tracking happiness can highlight problems with a value stream. For example, lack of staff happiness can be an important indicator of a problem with production, such as a missing automation that causes tedious manual work or a tangled architecture that makes coding new features difficult. High-performing organizations already measure employee engagement through metrics like the employee Net Promoter Score (eNPS). Notably for IT organizations, *Accelerate* also reports that employees in high-preforming organizations are 2.2 times more likely to recommend their organizations as great places to work.[7]

The eNPS has been a key part of growing Tasktop—I deployed it with my CFO years ago, and we continue to personally run the program in order to keep a pulse on any impediments to our teams' productivity and happiness. We deploy it with Fred Reichheld's approach of measuring the eNPS for each department, and we measure the average eNPS for all staff within each department.[8] This has provided invaluable feedback on when we need to place additional attention on a particular department.

However, when our deployment of the Flow Framework progressed outside of the product and engineering teams, a gap became apparent: we were only measuring eNPS within our organizational silos; we did not know what the eNPS was for a particular value stream. This is not to say that we did not track the happiness and engagement of staff within the value streams; the VP of Engineering and I dedicated significant time to this. But we found that we have value streams in different Management Zones. Our Hub product is in the Performance Zone, while several small initiatives exist in the Incubation Zone; and one of our major new initiatives exists in the Transformation Zone.

We have also found that it is essential to ensure that talent is assigned to the horizon in which they thrive. For example, some of our best developers thrive when solving the very hard-scale and performance problems deep in the platform. These developers tend to thrive in environments with well-specified constraints. In contrast, other developers thrive in the land of fuzzy front ends, rapid prototyping, and MVPs. Our VP of Engineering, like many other great engineering leads, has mastered assigning developers to the value streams in which they are likely to have the best shot at autonomy, mastery, and purpose.

But at one point, during a critical phase in a project where we were moving from the Incubation Zone to the Transformation Zone, we ended up with a mismatch. This mismatch negatively affected both the Hub team in the Performance Zone and the Transformation Zone teams, as the former had lost a critical contributor and the latter was not far enough along in product definition or architecture to help this top individual excel. It was impossible to spot this in the eNPS, because the engineering team was too large for the approximately twenty individuals impacted to make a visible dent in the eNPS score. It was through regular one-to-one meetings and the comment box within the eNPS survey that we saw something was wrong with the team structure.

The early warning system that the eNPS provided us previously—for example, seeing the scores dip when the wrong type of manager was put in charge of another department—was gone because we were measuring a silo. Yet for the Transformation Zone value stream, and for the great people doing the work on both sides, the effect of leaving the assignment as it was would have been highly detrimental. While metrics should never replace person-to-person conversations, at that moment, we realized that we were failing to follow the principles of the Flow Framework by measuring happiness only in functional silos and not within value streams.

Around this time, I met with Jon Smart, who had deployed a measurement of eNPS for each value stream at Barclays. I realized that Jon's approach to measuring engagement per value stream (not per functional silo) was what we were missing. We augmented our eNPS capture to specify not just the department but also the value stream. This visibility has turned out to be invaluable to understanding when the organization needs to do more to better support the teams working on the value streams, be that through better training or technical infrastructure.

Value Stream Dashboards

Correlating the flow metrics with business results provides us with a dashboard that connects the work being done in each value stream with the business results that the value stream is producing. This exercise forces the organization to define the boundaries of each value stream in terms of the teams and other costs, as well as mechanisms for deriving the results for each value stream, such as revenue and employee happiness. In Part III, we will look at the mechanisms needed to report these results directly from the systems underpinning the value stream. If a part of the value stream is excluded (e.g., people, activities, and costs that are upstream of developers), the flow metrics will not be correct; nor will they be meaningful if the value stream and product boundaries, as well as value metrics for each, are not accurately specified. But once we connect the Value Stream Metrics to the Value Stream Network, we get an unprecedented view of what flows through our software value streams and how that drives results, as visible in the mock-up of a value stream dashboard in Figure 5.2.

This sample dashboard provides a glimpse into how the Flow Framework can be used to track and manage a software product portfolio, and make the trade-offs that the business and IT make visible. For example, in the two value streams visible in Figure 5.2, it is instantly clear how much net new-business value, in the form of features, has flowed through each value stream.

Rather than setting a target for each value stream, the business sets a value metric, such as a revenue target for a particular product. The team responsible for the value stream can then set the corresponding flow distribution to optimize for feature flow. If a large amount of new risk work arrives during a critical time window (e.g., to implement a new regulatory requirement), the corresponding feature delivery reduction is visible to the key stakeholders through this dashboard. Similarly, if the development team for the product predicts that technical debt needs to be reduced in order to sustain the rate for feature delivery, those debts can be planned for and scheduled; and the trade-off between short-term and long-term impacts on feature velocity can be discussed and decided explicitly. This means that the same kind of trade-offs that product and engineering managers make at a much finer level of detail can cascade up to the business stakeholders at a higher level of abstraction, in order to drive adjustments and decisions.

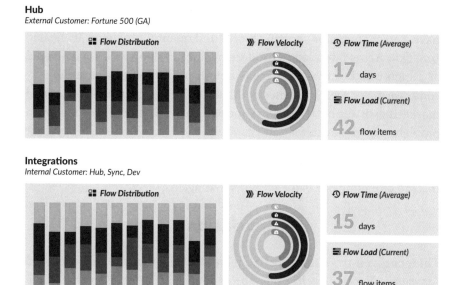

Figure 5.2: Sample Value Stream Dashboard

In addition, the business outcomes are accurate and visible to both the technical and the business stakeholders. Value Stream Networks are a complex dynamic system. Rather than blindly applying generic best practices, what Value Stream Metrics allow us to do is measure and then optimize the dynamic system specifically to our organization. For example, in the Hub story earlier, we witnessed that an accumulation of technical debt resulted in decreased flow velocity for features. For a different organization, that could have translated into increased flow time instead.

With the Flow Framework, we can determine these correlations using real data, and we can continually learn and adjust. If we see that too much flow distribution allocated to features is resulting in quality problems, we can determine whether that is likely to be a leading indicator for lost value in the form of revenue decline or user attrition. Common flow patterns will arise as well. For instance, an excessive flow load in a value stream will likely lead to lower flow velocity, but the point at which this happens will be particular to the value stream.

Finally, since all flow metrics are correlated to business results, we have a mechanism for spotting more fundamental problems. If the feature flow items intended to produce business value are being delivered at a high rate but that delivery is not translating into a revenue outcome, we may have a bottleneck outside of the value stream in sales and marketing; or the bottleneck may be external to the organization and a problem with product/market fit. While the Flow Framework does not propose hard rules for how to increase flow, it does make the effects of those dynamics visible so that we can manage our value streams instead of having our value streams manage us.

Conclusion

This chapter introduced a set of business results that should be tracked for each value stream in order to correlate investments in that value stream with outcome-based metrics. This set of outcomes can be further refined and expanded in ways that are particular to your business. But the goal of the Flow Framework is to ensure that there is at least one metric supporting each of the business results, and that each metric is tracked not only across the organization but for each value stream. In order to do that, the way that we think about both costs and value must be transitioned from a project-oriented model, which does not consider long-lived value streams, to a product-oriented model, where each value stream is aligned to the internal or external products that define our software and IT portfolios. (Architecting and configuring our tools to make this transition will be covered in Part III of this book.)

A measure of value is the canonical metric for each value stream. While this may seem obvious, just getting to the point where every product-oriented value stream and its customers are identified across the entire IT portfolio is a critical and missing piece in organizations. Once the product portfolio is defined, measuring cost, quality, and happiness are the other key pillars to aligning flow metrics to business results. Together, these metrics can be combined to create a value stream dashboard that opens up the black box of IT with a common set of Value Stream Metrics for both technologists and business leaders. With these in place, your organization can build on this minimal set to further inform decision making and support your strategy. You can create dashboards and reports that compare the profitability of mature value streams in the Performance Zone or you can ensure a very low flow time for feature delivery, which supports the experimentation and iteration needed in the Transformation Zone.

Before we move on to defining the Value Stream Network that supports this, we will review some large-scale and consequential digital transformations through the lens of the Flow Framework.

CHAPTER 6

Tracking Disruptions

L ike many others who have followed the evolution of companies as we neared and started progressing through the Turning Point of the Age of Software, I have witnessed organizations take debilitating turns that, in hindsight, seemed avoidable. In recent years, some of those failures have become increasingly visible to the mainstream press; for example, when the IT failures of Equifax caused a massive data breach in September 2017, or when British Airway's IT systems ground air traffic to a halt in May 2017. The leadership in both companies blamed IT and engineering, while tech industry pundits issued quotes that the old-guard leadership does not understand software and IT. What if we assume that both sides were trying their best to help the business win? What if the problem lay with a gap in information or perspective that prevented the understandings of one side to translate to the other?

In this chapter, we will review four software transformation stories through the lens of the Flow Framework. Instead of assuming malevolence or incompetence, we will assume that the leaders of these organizations, both on the technical and on the business side, were making the best decisions using the information and decision-making frameworks they had at hand. We will uncover how the flow of information and corresponding managerial approaches fell short. The chapter will conclude with a story of how these concepts can be used to turn the tide when navigating the transition through the Age of Software.

We'll start with a discussion of an industry-wide trend of defects in automotive software, and we'll explore how this is affecting the way that many carmakers need to think about flow distribution. Next, the Equifax security breach will serve as evidence of the disastrous outcomes that can occur when business leadership does not adequately plan for risks in key value streams. We'll revisit Nokia's fate, focusing on how the lack of understanding of debts at the executive level contributed to the company's downfall. Finally, we'll finish up with a success story, looking at how a deep level of understanding products, value streams, and flow have helped Microsoft navigate the entire Installation Period of the Age of Software.

BMW TRIP   First a Focus on Flow, Then on Automation

Frank and Rene lead me along the i3 line, which consists of the autonomous platforms moving the car from station to station every eight minutes.

"Since this is a modern line, we have been able to adopt some very new production technologies," Frank says. "Watch what happens to the electric drive here."

Frank points to a robot, which is very different looking than the large orange robots we had seen on the 1- and 2-Series lines. Each of those robots is entirely fenced in by a large cage. What we are seeing now is a blue-vested worker moving a large drive component into the car with the assistance of a robot.

"That is a new human-collaborative robot that we adopted for this line," Frank says. "It senses flesh and touch, and their control systems ensure they will never harm a human during operation."

Due to how cutting edge it is, in my ignorance I expected the i3 line to be completely automated by robots. Instead, I am watching what feels like a foreshadowing of the future, with a much closer level of human and machine collaboration than has previously been possible. Between the autonomous platforms and the human-collaborative robots, the continual learning, tuning, and optimization of the value streams is impressive.

"Over here, you will see that the i3 is split in two," Frank continues. "We have been able to parallelize the assembly of the two key parts of the car."

As we walk along the i3 line, Frank points to a very elaborate part of it, with taller robots than we had seen.

"This is a very interesting part of the line," Frank says. "This is where the split lines come together and where 'drive module' and 'life module' are glued to each other. The electric-car design has allowed us to assemble these parts separately until they come together at this workstation. Let's watch."

We walk to another catwalk and look down. I have not heard of the 'life module' before, but once one we move into view it is clear this is the part where humans sit. We watch as a line of glue is applied to the drive module and then the two parts of the car are pressed together by a massive robot. At this point I realize that, adding to my overall ignorance of mass production, I had no idea that glue technology has come this far.

It is clear that Frank and Rene are amused by my ongoing awe as they take me from one amazing workstation to another. All of this innovation on the i3 line, from the autonomous platforms to the parallelization of assembly, is incomprehensible to me at first. But seeing it the way Rene sees it—complete focus on flow—made all of these decisions and optimizations start to slowly make sense: they start with end-to-end-flow thinking and keep optimizing each step and sequence to improve the time and velocity of that flow.

We turn a corner, and the skeleton of an i8 appears in the distance . . .

Defects versus Features in Automotive Software

The amount of software in automobiles has been on a rapid rise since 2010.[1] With car manufacturing in a phase of maturity, competition between carmakers has been driving leading manufacturers to move beyond styling and performance specifications to gain market share. In the Age of Software, much of that competitive advantage has shifted to infotainment systems, connected mobility solutions, and autonomous driving features. All of this means more software.

Cars have been evolving from one million lines of code for basic drive features, such as traction control; to ten million lines of code for increasing digitization, growth of electronic control units, and additional control software complexity introduced by electric cars; to one hundred million lines of code with the growth of the connected vehicle and infotainment; and soon, to one billion lines of code with the advent of autonomous drive.[2]

This fast rate of scaling has resulted in some interesting consequences. The Stout Risius Ross, Inc. (SRR) *Automotive Warranty & Recall Report* for 2016 highlights the trend of software-related recalls and their growth in Figure 6.1.

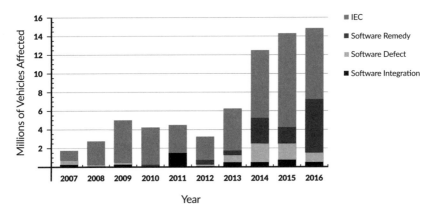

Figure 6.1: Recalls of Electronic Car Components in the United States[3]

Contains data for BMW, Daimler AG, FCA, Ford, General Motors, Honda, Hyundai, Kia Toyota, Volkswagen, and Volvo. Identified from data set updated through 2016. Excludes Takata Inflator recall campaigns.

In total, fourteen million recalls occurred due to software-related issues in 2016, according to SRR.[4] This growth in recalls is problematic for the automotive industry, as more and more of the customer's experience with a car is defined by the quality of the software. (Note that these statistics predate any broad adoption of autonomous drive systems, where the consequences of software defects can be even more severe.)

The current state of the automotive industry illustrates a transition between the Deployment Period of the Age of Mass Production and the Turning Point of the Age of Software. When the automotive industry was in the Installation Period of the Age of Mass Production, from 1908 until 1929, cars had constant quality problems.[5] Edwards Deming famously created a management system that resulted in Lean, Six Sigma, and other methods that succeeded at getting car quality under control.[6] Other than exceptional events, such as the Takata airbag failure in 2016, manufacturing quality and delivery remain a solved problem and a shining example of the manufacturing maturity that coalesces in the Deployment Period.

However, it no longer matters if all mechanical aspects of a car function with high reliability if a software component fails and causes the car to shut down and require towing. What I believe we are seeing in the increased recall rates is the result of the Operating Model disruption of the car industry. Due to the car becoming a digital and connected experience that's expected to meet the customer's mobility needs in innovative new ways, like car sharing, there is tremendous pressure for car manufacturers to bring new features to market.

Through the lens of the Flow Framework, we know that there is a zero-sum game in the number of features added, defects fixed, and risks mitigated. Across the automotive industry, we have seen the quality trade-off that results from features taking precedence over other flow items. This is not to say that prioritizing feature flow at the expense of quality is always bad. For example, in the early scaling days of internet-scale companies such as Twitter, outages and other quality problems were common; yet that product succeeded in winning its market. However, the trade-off must be done with forward-looking business consequences in mind, and the recall rate suggests that the various software components in the car need to start shifting the flow distribution accordingly.

In sophisticated software delivery environments, this is not always easy and may require setting up entire internal value streams related to quality. For instance, when I visited the hardware and software labs of a company that creates inverter software for electric cars, I was amazed to learn that over one thousand software engineers are involved with inverter production. Just creating the simulation software that is required to ensure that the inverter never delivers a spike of electricity that causes an electric car to accelerate at the wrong time is a large feat, especially when you consider any of the thousands of electrical components that degrade and malfunction over the life span of the car. Similarly, the BMW Group has created a set of value streams for end-to-end car simulation that runs on supercomputers in Iceland.[7] They have leveraged the principles of DevOps to create a continuous integration system that simulates both the software and the hardware behaviors of a car. Even at Tasktop, we have an internal value stream for complex customer value stream simulation, as our integration tests cannot exhaustively test all customer-tool configuration scenarios.

In each of these examples, it became clear to the organization that enabling fast flow velocity and reducing flow time for features required novel investments in embedding quality into the value streams, which happened at the cost of feature delivery in the near term. The Flow Framework hypothesis here is that too much flow distribution has been allocated to features and has resulted in too much technical debt, implying that future releases need a focus on defect fixes and reducing debts until the recall rates stabilize.

Risk Problems at Equifax

The security of a software system is related to the surface area that it exposes. The larger the scale of the system, and the more web services and other internet-facing capabilities it exposes, the more work is involved in protecting it. A key trend in the Deployment Period of the Age of Software is that traditional businesses are bringing more systems online. As new web-based offerings are deployed for customers and business partners, this footprint increases.

Cybersecurity is a software "arms race" between companies managing IT and software infrastructures that protect sensitive data and bad actors who create infrastructure and software to break through those protections. Since the start of the Turning Point in 2000, security breaches have been soaring, in both number of incidents and consumers affected.[8] Breeches that made the headlines include those at Home

Depot, Target, and JP Morgan Chase, each of which resulted in over fifty million accounts compromised in total.[9] While these breaches have shaken consumer confidence about these organizations' ability to provide reliable security of their personal data, the 2017 Equifax breach had even broader implications.

Since its founding in the United States in 1899, Equifax has been storing financial and other private data for its US customers. When Equifax was breached in 2017, approximately 145.5 million consumer accounts were compromised.[10] In other words, for a business that had mastered its core function—data protection—in the previous age, during the Turning Point, the company management presided over decisions that led to this vast breach of the company's core asset.

The CEO of Equifax lost his job, and a congressional hearing followed. In that hearing, the CEO blamed the breach on a single developer.[11] Having a technology company CEO blame an individual contributor for this—for an oversight that happened during the course of daily work—is unconscionable. From a technologist's point of view, it is as unthinkable as the idea of the CEO of a car company attempting to publicly blame a single assembly worker for the recall of all vehicles produced by a plant. Car company CEOs have a clear understanding of the needs for safety and security to be a systemic and robust part of production processes. In contrast, Equifax's CEO's statements underscore the scope of disconnect between traditional business management and the means of production in the Age of Software.

Let's assume that the Equifax leadership had the success of their business and shareholders in mind when steering the company into the extremely vulnerable position in which it found itself in 2017. We can reasonably assume that the CEO did not want to lose his job, and that the leadership did not want to irreparably tarnish their own reputations and that of the company brand. The role of company leadership is to direct and protect the business, as Equifax had been doing for over a hundred years. This implies that something so fundamental changed during Equifax's digital transformation that it became impossible for the CEO and company leadership to do their jobs. The software systems had to be scaled in a way that the leadership and management could not keep up with.

So, what was Equifax prioritizing ahead of security? Was it faster delivery of new features and services to remain competitively viable against their key competition? Was it an increase in the quality of some critical parts of the application portfolio? Whichever trade-off was made, in hindsight, it is clear that work on risks was not getting enough allocation in the value stream, with infrequent reviews and a lack of prioritization.[12] Given the pressure to deliver new digital offerings so many companies feel when competing with tech giants and startups, perhaps a focus on customer-visible features and quality resulted in the deprioritization of risks, while leadership lacked visibility into the level of debts that was accumulating on the backlogs for the delivery teams. Whatever the source of the imbalance in flow distribution, the result was disastrous, both for the company and for the US citizens that it served.

An important property of flow distribution is that it cascades up, from delivery teams to business strategy; we can measure flow distribution for one value stream or consider the impact of the combined flow distribution across all of an organization's value streams. Given the level of security risk that a series of technology decisions exposed Equifax to, we can hypothesize that the CEO should have allocated the majority of the company's value streams to focus on risks and debts.

Empowering management with the visibility and understanding of which flow distribution investments will support strategic goals, be that securing digital products or enabling future feature velocity, is how we need to connect the language and reality of IT to the business. Had the CEO of Equifax understood this, he may have had the opportunity to create a north star of risk reduction across the company's value streams. The Flow Framework hypothesis here is that Equifax failed due to a lack of risk and debt prioritization on key value streams.

Debts and the Downfall of Nokia

Low product quality, low feature velocity, and security risks are familiar to us because we have experienced each as consumers of digital offerings. The continuation of the Nokia story revolves around the much less visible effect of debts on value streams and company success.

Nokia was founded in 1865 in Finland. The company started as a pulp mill, then turned into a rubber business, and subsequently shifted to electronics in the mid-twentieth century. Nokia was born in the Age of Steel and made an amazing pivot into the Age of Mass Production, putting it at the helm of the mobile revolution. Then, while armed with the best handsets and dominant mobile operating system at the time, it failed to make the transition to the Age of Software.

I met with the CIO of Symbian in 2008. Symbian created the operating system adopted by Nokia for its phones. Nokia acquired the company in 2008.[13] I founded Tasktop a year earlier and learned that Nokia was interested in the commercial extensions to our open-source developer productivity tool. A meeting with the CIO resulted in our first six-figure software sale, which bought us another few months of life as an early-stage, bootstrapped startup. But that was not the most valuable part of the meeting.

I had spent a decade in academia, industry research, and open-source development; but at that point in my career, I had never spent any significant time interacting with an IT leader who had over a thousand IT staff reporting to them. From the two-hour meeting, I developed a profound respect for the Symbian CIO and had the opportunity to empathize with his challenges. Everything that seemed easy and obvious to me, with my experiences working on high-velocity teams, was very different in his much-larger-scaled world. While I had spent plenty of time working with technical complexity, both from a source code and a computational point of view, I had never encountered this level of value stream complexity directly. I also learned of a form of technical debt that I did not know existed.

Ward Cunningham established the concept of technical debt back in 1992.[14] I learned about it in 1999 while working on the AspectJ programming language team at Xerox PARC, where Jim Hugunin, the technical lead, ensured that we dedicated a portion of our flow for each release to reducing technical debt. Jim treated technical debt as first-class work that we should give attention to in order to make sure our platform did not get too difficult to update and maintain. Reducing technical debt became part of our daily work. What the Symbian CIO was dealing with (and in a later discussion, the CTO) was related, but at a scale that went far beyond the code.

In the 1990s, the Symbian Series 40 OS introduced me to the possibilities of mobile computing. Through the acquisition of Symbian, Nokia sent a signal that the future of the mobile experience was not just elegant hardware but also software. By 2008, Symbian was installed on the majority of mobile devices.[15] Nokia, a master of the Age of Mass Production, had acquired a company born into the early part of the Age of Software.

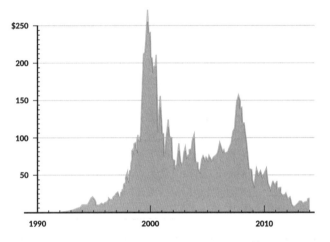

Figure 6.2: The Rise and Fall of Nokia[16]

The race was on to enhance the software experience. Under Nokia, Symbian was crafting the next generation Series 60 OS. The new OS needed to deliver a whole new set of features that would connect the mobile device to the pent-up demand of mobile services and commerce.

When a software organization runs fast to bring new features to market, compromises are made. Symbian had an amazing reputation for quality. Their risk and security practices, which I got to review firsthand, were far ahead of their time. So what kind of work suffers when the business sets a high bar for quality and security while recognizing that new features are critical to the growing market? The answer is the work that is needed to take down debt. This includes technical debt, infrastructure debt, and debts that accumulate in the Value Stream Network itself, such as automation gaps that impede developer productivity and flow. (Figure 6.2 illustrates Nokia's fall from a $250 billion market cap to this devastating outcome for all involved.)

Fast forward to 2013: Nokia has lost its place in the market and has been purchased for $7.2 billion by Microsoft.[17] Shortly before this purchase, the new CEO of Nokia, Stephen Elop, released the "burning platform" memo to his staff:

> There is a pertinent story about a man who was working on an oil platform in the North Sea. He woke up one night from a loud explosion, which suddenly set his entire oil platform on fire. In mere moments, he was surrounded by flames. Through the smoke and heat, he barely made his way out of the chaos to the platform's edge. When he looked down over the edge, all he could see were the dark, cold, foreboding Atlantic waters.
>
> As the fire approached him, the man had mere seconds to react. He could stand on the platform, and inevitably be consumed by the burning flames. Or, he could plunge thirty meters in to the freezing waters. The man was standing upon a "burning platform," and he needed to make a choice.
>
> He decided to jump. It was unexpected. In ordinary circumstances, the man would never consider plunging into icy waters. But these were not ordinary times—his platform was on fire. The man survived the fall and the waters. After he was rescued, he noted that a "burning platform" caused a radical change in his behavior.
>
> We, too, are standing on a "burning platform," and we must decide how we are going to change our behavior.
>
> Over the past few months, I've shared with you what I've heard from our shareholders, operators, developers, suppliers and from

you. Today, I'm going to share what I've learned and what I have come to believe.

I have learned that we are standing on a burning platform.

And, we have more than one explosion—we have multiple points of scorching heat that are fueling a blazing fire around us.

For example, there is intense heat coming from our competitors, more rapidly than we ever expected. Apple disrupted the market by redefining the smartphone and attracting developers to a closed, but very powerful ecosystem . . .[18]

At this time, many a rumor was floated on the reasons for Nokia's downfall. At one point, a colleague told me a story about seeing a Finnish newspaper that had put the face of a single Nokia engineer on the front page, asserting that the calamity that fell on the Finnish economy was "his fault" because he suggested that Nokia hold off on a capacitive touchscreen model. I was not able to substantiate my friend's story, but this does go toward illustrating how far the rumors and blame mongering went.

True or not, singling out a single engineer—reminiscent of the CEO of Equifax—creates a blame-oriented culture, making the change and risk-taking that is critical to navigating the Turning Point difficult. Also, having this blame come from senior leadership is nonsensical when viewed from the vantage point of a mature production system. A single decision or mistake by a single staff member should not be able to bring down a hundred-plus-year-old company. Yet this blame on a single engineer seems to have happened in both cases.

Let's assume that Nokia's leadership sought success for the company and its shareholders. Once again, something was missing from their calculus on how best to direct and protect the company. Stephen Elop's memo may have been an epitaph to a foregone conclusion. But when I first read it, it cemented for me what I heard from Nokia engineers: the Symbian Series 60 OS had accumulated a mountain of technical debt— something that Nokia management was not familiar with due to the much simpler Series 40 OS. It was a level of debt that went well beyond the source code and architecture; it had actually transcended the source code and seeped into the entire value stream and the management and planning of their software delivery. That kind of debt simply was not present in the Series 40 OS, which was created at a time when technologists were running the organization. Stephen Elop had come from Microsoft, an organization that understood technical debt, and he saw the problem at both the technical and the business level.

Whether Elop identified the problem too late, or placed a bet on a fundamentally flawed mobile platform, or whether the Nokia organization was too broken by that point to correct course, is less clear. But what if Nokia had discovered their technical debt problem years earlier, similar to how in 2002, Apple discovered that the technical debt in their Mac OS 9 could not be refactored away? Instead, Apple realized that their next operating system, Mac OS X, had to be recreated from the ground up.[19]

From my experience and interviews with Nokia staff, my belief is that the fate of Nokia would not have changed dramatically if they'd had a capacitive touchscreen in their hands well before Apple did. At a business level, Nokia had not prioritized reducing technical debt before it accumulated to the point where the platform could no longer evolve to meet the business's needs. It was impossible to position the company for a shift from the world of mass-produced buttons to a software-powered screen. The Flow Framework hypothesis here is that feature flow was so inhibited by the debt and the existing architecture that the platform had reached a dead end. Investment in a new platform was required before the runway and capital for replatforming ran out.

Product Delivery at Microsoft

The Equifax and Nokia stories detail the existential threats that can result from company leadership not having the right visibility and understanding of the nature of large-scale software delivery. But what about examples of the opposite? We have the recent digital natives, like Netflix and Google, but these may be less relatable due to how little debt relatively young digital organizations have within their IT portfolios.

This lack of legacy is not entirely a coincidence. For instance, Google has been a shining example of product-oriented management in terms of the number of customer-facing products that it has sunset. But Microsoft, a company that helped start the Age of Software, is an even more interesting example due to the much longer time frame that it has had to accumulate legacy and scale.

Unlike some of the younger tech giants, Microsoft has had plenty of opportunity to pile up unsurmountable amounts of technical debt, build up software complexity that would bring features to a halt, and create a massive surface area for security attacks that could have had them lose the market when the severity and sophistication of attacks increased. However, Microsoft has a fundamental advantage in how it manages its software portfolio: it has been product-oriented from the outset.

In 2003, I spent six months working directly for Charles Simonyi, former Chief Architect of Microsoft, at his startup, Intentional Software. Over the long days and evenings, Charles told me countless stories of how Bill Gates and the Microsoft leadership approached managing and evolving the company portfolio. It was Gates's shift to the internet that I found most surprising and impressive.

In 1995, Gates realized that if Microsoft did not dramatically increase its delivery of internet-centric features, the company's place in the future was far from certain.[20] He then set the vision for Microsoft's value streams to prioritize internet-centric features in order to play disruption defense against Netscape. The quality and technical debt issues that resulted were clear to anyone frustrated by early releases of Internet Explorer; but these were deliberate decisions, and those debts were paid off afterward. Gates was able to allocate flow distribution in a potentially counterintuitive way, as the quality issues that resulted had a non-trivial impact on the brand of Microsoft. In the end, it was that trade-off that secured Microsoft's future into the Turning Point and growth of the internet.

What happened next was even more impressive. Consider Gates's memo that follows, which was sent to the whole company, and note that it is dated in 2002, far before security breaches were making the headlines that they do today.

From: Bill Gates
Sent: Tuesday, January 15, 2002 5:22 PM
To: Microsoft and Subsidiaries: All FTE
Subject: Trustworthy Computing

Every few years I have sent out a memo talking about the highest priority for Microsoft. Two years ago, it was the kickoff of our .NET strategy. Before that, it was several memos about the importance of the Internet to our future and the ways we could make the Internet truly useful for people. Over the last year it has become clear that ensuring .NET is a platform for Trustworthy Computing is more important than any other part of our work. If we don't do this, people simply will not be willing—or able—to take advantage of all the other great work we do. Trustworthy Computing is the highest priority for all the work we are doing. We must lead the industry to a whole new level of Trustworthiness in computing.

. . . What I mean by this is that customers will always be able to rely on these systems to be available and to secure their information. Trustworthy Computing is computing that is as available, reliable and secure as electricity, water services and telephony.

Today, in the developed world, we do not worry about electricity and water services being available. With telephony, we rely both on its availability and its security for conducting highly confidential business transactions without worrying that information about who we call or what we say will be compromised. Computing falls well short of this, ranging from the individual user who is not willing to add a new application because it might destabilize their system, to a corporation that moves slowly to embrace e-business because today's platforms do not make the grade.

The events of last year—from September's terrorist attacks to a number of malicious and highly publicized computer viruses— reminded every one of us how important it is to ensure the integrity and security of our critical infrastructure, whether it's the airlines or computer systems.

Computing is already an important part of many people's lives. Within 10 years, it will be an integral and indispensable part of almost everything we do. Microsoft and the computer industry will only succeed in that world if CIOs, consumers and everyone else sees that Microsoft has created a platform for Trustworthy Computing.[21]

Just as Gates had steered the ship to feature delivery when that pivot was needed, he reset the course across all company value streams to reducing risk through the Trustworthy Computing initiative; and he did so years before security issues became a common headline in popular press. Recognizing the Nokia-level severity of technical debt problems that resulted in the "blue screen of death" associated with the Windows operating system and the 1990s "DLL hell,"[22] Gates recruited one of the most talented programming language and software architects in the industry, offering Anders Hejlsberg a $3 million signing bonus in 1996 to help create a much more robust developer platform.[23]

Analyzing these actions through the lens of the Flow Framework indicates how Gates gave the organizational north star of first focusing on risk, then focusing on debt, and how he recognized that turning those dials up to ten meant turning the feature dial down to zero. While we can retroactively analyze his actions and those of Simonyi using the Flow Framework, Gates and Simonyi did not need it. Both had the programming and product background required to understand software delivery and IT in its native language, as has Satya Nadella with his leadership of Microsoft into the cloud.

I had the opportunity to fly on Simonyi's private jet and spend weeks programming on his 270-foot yacht. My key takeaway from that experience was that in the Age of Software, for wealth to be shared across the economy, we need this kind of strategic decision-making framework to be available to all business leaders.

Conclusion

When walking the BMW Group Leipzig production line, I was struck by the sheer scale and excellence of the infrastructure before my eyes. Imagine one of the largest buildings in the world with more machines working in unison than you have ever seen before. The coordinated chorus that you see is not static; it's directly wired into the needs of the business and the changes of market. If too many cars appear in the rework area, the plant director and other staff will instantly see it and redirect resources to address the quality issue. If more demand for the i3 comes up, more automation or parallelization can be deployed to that line in order to increase the volume of output. If a new feature is desired for the i8, it's bespoke production line can adjust accordingly.

There is so much similarity between the infrastructure for innovation of the BMW Group and what Microsoft created that the answer must lie in the way that the business and the means of production are connected in these high-performing organizations. With Nokia's downfall, the problem was not that the developers were unaware that the debts around the platform were crippling innovation; the problem was that the business did not see it, and as a result, could not plan around the implications.

I lived through a similar event at Tasktop, with the success of Tasktop Sync becoming a debt-ridden dead end, requiring us to create a new platform with Hub. Though the replatforming itself was painful, it was a tractable technical problem. The hard part was—and is—having a decision-making framework that enables company leadership to know when holding off on replatforming is likely to result in company death or decline.

Bill Gates and the leadership at Microsoft have software engineering backgrounds; as such, these decisions and their impact on the business are probably innate to them. It is the ability to make these trade-offs at the business level that has helped some companies thrive while others falter. The disproportionately large number of developers at the helm of today's tech giants may be related to the firsthand view that software development provides in understanding the flow of features, defects, risks, and debts.

This kind of training is not dissimilar to what we saw in the past Deployment Period. For example, the majority of the BMW Group's CEOs were originally plant managers.[24] A plant manager intuitively knows how to connect production flow to the business strategy. They start their career doing that for a single value stream, then for an entire plant; finally, they learn enough along the way to do it for the entire company.

While this plays nicely into the role that developers increasingly play as "the new kingmakers,"[25] elevating the subset of developers who are interested in leadership is not enough. We need to elevate the practice of software delivery by connecting today's business leaders and technologists and reducing that chasm, not broadening it. To do that, we need a common language that empowers both the technologists and the business stakeholders with the right kind of information to drive good decision making for the business.

In this chapter, we explored stories of critically flawed decision making that resulted from the business not having the right level of visibility into software delivery, and how easy it becomes for business leaders with the best of intentions to misguide the company into peril. What the Microsoft story showed us is that there is a better way. The Flow Framework encompasses some of the key aspects of that new approach to managing organizations through the Turning Point.

Conclusion to Part II

In Part II, Value Stream Metrics were introduced, which are meant to bridge the gap between the business and IT. Connecting what flows through our value streams to business outcomes through flow metrics is how we will get the kind of visibility and feedback with IT that the BMW Group has with its advanced manufacturing lines. The key aspects of Value Stream Metrics covered in Part II include:

- **Defining flow items:** Each flow item can be measured by observing the tool network. With the flow items, we can measure the flow of business value through the tool network and correlate that to business results.

- **Setting the flow distribution:** This is the most consequential aspect of the Flow Framework, as all other metrics rely on it. We need to track the target flow distribution for each product's value stream to determine what type of business value is being delivered.
- **Measuring flow velocity:** We need to be able to measure the magnitude of each flow item being delivered to the customer over time. This is the flow velocity, and it is adapted from the concept of velocity in Agile software development.
- **Tracking flow time:** Flow distribution and flow velocity provide an empirical measure of how much of which kind of work was done over a period of time, but they do not indicate how quickly that work cycled through the system. Flow time defines the speed at which we are delivering business value to the market.
- **Measuring flow load:** In order to optimize flow in a value stream, we need to avoid overutilizing the value stream by having too much work in progress (WIP). The flow load metric allows us to track this at the value stream level (e.g., by indicating how many features are being worked on in parallel).
- **Tracking flow efficiency:** Within each product's value stream, flow items are either being worked on or waiting for work to be done or for dependencies to be addressed. Flow efficiency measures the ratio of productive to waiting time, enabling the tuning of our value streams for productivity.
- **Connecting to business results:** Value, cost, quality, and happiness are the four buckets of business results that need to be tracked as part of the Flow Framework in order to correlate software investment with business performance, and to provide a common set of results-oriented metrics to connect the business with IT.

As we enter the Deployment Period, organizations cannot wait for technologists to rise through the ranks. The cautionary tales in Chapter 6 indicate that too many businesses will be lost at too large a cost to their staff and to the economy as a whole if business leaders do not adapt. To avoid the next Equifax and Nokia, we need a common language and framework to connect today's technology and business leaders. Our organizations' collective ability to understand how business value flows through software delivery, and how to predict and adapt these flows to thrive through market changes, will be what enables competitiveness and success in the Age of Software.

The question now is how do we do this? How do we get this elusive level of visibility and feedback into software delivery? Most enterprise IT organizations have tried every dashboard, business intelligence, and big data solution out there, so why is it that IT remains a black box to the business?

The answer is that we need to connect the new means of production directly, which requires creating a Value Stream Network. This is the infrastructure layer that makes software delivery within digital organizations so dramatically different to the companies that fumbled the future. In Part III, we will learn how to create this new kind of network to connect the business to software delivery.

PART III

Flow Framework™

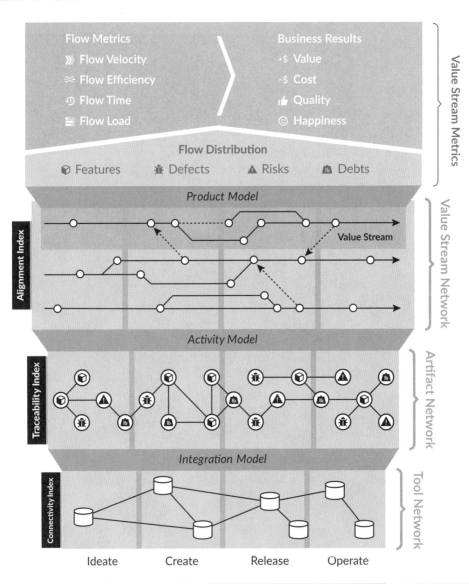

PART III

VALUE STREAM NETWORKS

W e need a new kind of infrastructure for connecting software delivery to the business and aligning our organizations around product-oriented value streams. In Part III, we will define this new concept of a Value Stream Network, the three layers of the network, indices for measuring the network, and the model that underpins it.

As we will see in Chapter 7, the need to create a Value Stream Network is rooted in the explosion of best-of-breed and specialized tools that have grown through the Agile and DevOps movements. In the world of the single-tool platform pioneered by, IBM Rational, the entire Value Stream Network is inherently connected. This is the very model that has been emulated by tech giants such as Google and Microsoft. For example, Microsoft reports 3,500 people working in its Developer Division, with 800 people dedicated to Visual Studio Team Services (VSTS).[1] Considering this level of staffing, we can extrapolate that over the years tech giants like Microsoft have invested billions into creating in-house tool networks that provide end-to-end flow and feedback across their value streams. That has given them a seemingly insurmountable advantage when compared to enterprises who are using best-of-breed vendors and open-source tools that were never designed to provide this level of value stream flow or feedback to the business.

The end-to-end grip of Rational on enterprise tool networks has been disrupted and replaced by a new breed of highly tailored best-of-breed tools from hundreds of vendors and open-source projects. As summarized by the findings in *Accelerate*, tool choice comes with productivity benefits for individual stakeholders.[2] But this heterogeneity also comes with a cost, as flow and feedback are thwarted by disparate tools.

To survive the resulting environmental chaos and move from project to product to gain visibility over our value streams, we have two choices: either we undertake the kind of billion-dollar investments that the tech giants have undertaken into creating a unified tool suite or we need to connect off-the-shelf tools produced by vendors and open-source projects into a Value Stream Network. Without a connected Value Stream Network, flow metrics cannot work, as they would only show data for segments of the value stream, not end-to-end flows. This puts organizations back into the pitfalls of local optimizations of the value stream that we saw in the failure stories of Part II. The Value Stream Network is the missing layer that's needed to connect the various software delivery functions to each other and to the business.

In Part III, we will cover:

- *The fundamental shift in the technology landscape that necessitates Value Stream Networks as a first-class layer of the IT stack*
- *A summary of the study of 308 tool networks that provides evidence for the way that information needs to flow across tools in the Value Stream Network*
- *An overview of each layer of the network, and the Integration Model, Activity Model, and Product Model that connect the layers to each other and to the business*
- *The three epiphanies that led to the concept of Value Stream Networks and how each provides us with the guidance for*

implementing flow, feedback, and continuous learning within our organizations

This part of the book will shift from the reasons why businesses need a new framework to what you need to track, measure, and define in order to achieve the flow, feedback, and continual learning provided by the Flow Framework.

CHAPTER 7

The Ground Truth of Enterprise Tool Networks

Before we dive into understanding how to create and connect a Value Stream Network, we must first understand the ground truth of enterprise IT tool networks. In a car plant, finding the ground truth is easy, as we can see the cars flowing along the production line. In software delivery, we are dealing with knowledge work, which is considered invisible. However, if our understanding of the universe were limited to what we could observe with our eyes, we would not have made it past the Age of Steam and Railways. Just as we need tools to see how electricity flows through a grid or factory, we also need a new approach to see how knowledge work flows through the tools in which software collaboration and knowledge creation are tracked.

In this chapter, we will start with another visit to the BMW Group plant to seek inspiration in the ground truth of car production. We will then shift back to see how these concepts of visibility might apply in enterprise tool networks, and why it is important, not just for developers but for all levels of leadership, to understand the ground truth of software delivery. This does not imply that everyone needs to learn how to code any more than I had to learn the intricacies of advanced manufacturing to appreciate the BMW Group's mastery of mass production. But every-one wanting to make sound decisions around IT and software investment must understand software delivery at the level of business value flow.

This chapter will start by demonstrating how we can take a virtual Gemba walk (a Japanese term that refers to the personal observation of work) of our value streams by inspecting the artifacts in our tool networks. Then we will take a closer look at what the ground truth of a developer's activity is like when their work is disconnected from the value stream. Finally, we will dive into more detail on my first two epiphanies. The first epiphany stemmed from measuring the massive productivity loss from developers working disconnected from the value stream. The second epiphany is that this problem is not particular for developers but relates to all technology and business stakeholders involved in the value stream.

BMW TRIP Tailoring the Lines to the Business

While I have never owned a BMW, I have long respected the brand as a pinnacle of car design and engineering. And nothing embodies the combination of those two things for me more than the i8. The moment images of it started surfacing on the internet in 2014, it became my desktop wallpaper—not because I desired one but because I was fascinated by how such a wonder of technology could be built.

"As you can see, this is, by far, the shortest line," Frank says. "Each of the workers is much more of a generalist, as they perform multiple steps with much less automation happening on the production line. We have much more flexibility here."

We proceed to walk down the i8 production line. With a thirty-minute takt time, we are walking much faster than the cars are moving along the line, not the other way around. This makes for an interesting and slow visual progression of watching as each car flips from current to future states as we progress from one workstation to the next.

But even with all its technological and design grandeur, I keep losing focus on the i8 line and looking back to the i3 line. It feels like I should be more excited by the i8 production, as I have always thought of it as the more impressive product. But what's even more impressive here is the production itself, the complexity and intricacy of which seems orders of magnitude more complex than the cars themselves. I realize that it is the production that impresses me more than the product, and I veer back to the i3 line.

I am still thinking about what Frank told me about the autonomous platforms that carried the i3s down the line.

"Frank, I've been meaning to ask," I say while watching an i3 nearing completion, moving along on its platform. "Can you reconfigure the routes these platforms take?"

"Yes, we can," Frank replies. "For example, once we started producing hybrid i3s, we were able to create new routings. The autonomous platforms can be configured through software," he explains. "But that does not happen often."

That does not happen often. That statement keeps circling through my mind as we start to make our way back toward the 1- and 2-Series production lines. We see some more amazing things along the way, including new prototype bodies, test centers where sample cars accelerate on rollers to over two hundred kilometers per hour (about 124 miles per hour), and water tightness testing where cars are drenched in simulations of a torrential downpour. This is reminiscent enough of James Bond walking through Q's lab that part of me expects to turn the corner and see a BMW shooting flames from its underbelly, frying the crash-test dummies standing beside it.

My mind is fascinated by what I see: on one side a low-variability and high-volume 1- and 2-Series line, and on the other, a higher-variability and lower-volume i8 line. And this very strange thing of an i3 line that can be reconfigured to add something as complex as a hybrid engine to the production process.

A year earlier, when I visited the Bosch gasoline/hybrid lab, I got a sense of just how complex a modern hybrid is; some of my colleagues likened it to the complexity of two cars in one. Somehow, this kind of change could be handled by the plant. But the role of the plant was to produce cars at the volume targeted by their respective value streams. And even though each car rolling off the line was unique, the design of the cars did not change fundamentally, since the cars were not designed during the production process.

Was this a better way of conceptualizing how large-scale software should be built? How could we gain this kind of visibility into the software production process?

"Mik," Frank says, snapping me out of my recursion of conundrums. "Shall we go for coffee?"

"Yes," I mutter. Rene nods and smiles at me, clearly pleased to see how the experience has gotten to me. This plant means a lot to him, as he started his career here before moving to IT. And I finally understand why.

"Okay," Frank says. "Now you will finally get to see the bottleneck."

Looking for Ground Truth

In the 1980s, the automotive industry was suffering a well-documented quality crisis.[1] Cars had become more complex, production scaled up, and quality problems ensued. Producing cars was already a solved problem; however, producing cars at scale, within the constraints of competitive dynamics, turned out to be another problem altogether. It is a story the industry witnessed again with the challenges that Tesla had scaling up Model 3 production.[2]

It was the Lean movement that got the quality and variability aspects of production under control at scale. One of the fundamental parts of Lean management is the concept of the Gemba walk.[3] The point is to see firsthand where value is created and to connect company leadership to the ground truth of production. My visit to the BMW plant was a privileged invitation to embark on a two-day Gemba walk. The reason I sensed how much I would learn from that Gemba walk is that over the past decade, I have been taken on dozens of other walks of this sort through Fortune 500 IT organization offices, as well as those of software startups and so-called unicorns (privately held startups valued at over $1 billion).

While large TVs that radiate all sorts of dashboards and telemetry are increasingly common, they all look different. They lack a common business-level language for showing what's flowing through the software value streams. Gemba walks, on the other hand, are visceral and are so effective in manufacturing because all the work and all the infrastructure supporting the work is visible.

While software may be more ephemeral than cars and parts, the use of software tools presents a uniquely accurate and fine-grained way to view and analyze how software itself is built. Nearly every action taken by a software developer is tracked in one or more tools. With the right set of models and abstractions, it is possible to analyze all of that data. This is a level of data capture and fidelity that even manufacturing would be envious of, as few disciplines have as much work activity externalized into a tool repository. Given the maturity of the discipline of information visualization, we should be able to visualize every aspect of each activity that happens within a software value stream. As such, the question is not whether or not we can visualize software delivery; the question is how do we visualize and model that data to be meaningful to the business.

The majority of my career as a researcher has been dedicated to creating tools that connect developer activity with the flow of work in the value stream. The data in tool repositories is the ground truth of software delivery. In this chapter, we are going to do a virtual Gemba walk through the discoveries that my colleagues and I made as we collected and analyzed that data. It is through these discoveries that the three epiphanies summarized in Chapter 1 came upon me, each revealing a new aspect of what Value Stream Networks are and how we can use them to get true end-to-end visibility into software production.

A Dev Day in the Life: The First Epiphany

My very first Gemba walk of a developer's daily work involved walking through my own daily work. It was out of sheer desperation. I was in the early stages of my own programming career at Xerox PARC; it was 2002; and AspectJ, our open-source project, was starting to hit its stride. Our user community was thriving at the time. We had continuous delivery in place, were following Kent Beck's XP methodologies, and had the ambitious plan of making a mark on the landscape of programming languages.

The constant stream of defects and feature requests submitted by our growing open-source community, along with our desire to fulfill them and get onto the next set of language or tool features, resulted in a seemingly endless backlog of work. We knew that our ability to organically grow a programming community around our new language was directly proportional to the flow time and flow velocity of features that we added. This translated into my first foray into regular seventy- to eighty-hour work weeks. Living in San Francisco and commuting to Palo Alto also meant that I'd sleep under my office desk at least once during the two-week public-release cycle, which resulted in even more hands-on-keyboard time. My boss, Gregor Kiczales, then one of the designers of the Common Lisp Object System (CLOS), told our team that you get to stand on the ground floor of a technical breakthrough only once—or very rarely, twice—in a career. That poured more fuel on the fire.

Then the pain started. At first, I ignored the dull ache in my forearms. But with the inevitable frenzy of features to complete for the next release and my excitement about getting them out release after release, the pain got worse. By 2002, each mouse click hurt, and the scheduled breaks all seemed like one step forward and two steps back. Xerox PARC had a staff nurse, who recognized that I had a repetitive strain injury (RSI) consisting of inflamed tendons and nerves in my forearms. She created a plan for me, which boiled down to taking four extra-strength ibuprofen per day for two months to reduce the inflammation. The two months passed, my arms felt slightly better, but as soon as I got off the ibuprofen, the pain seemed worse than ever before. She prescribed me two wrist splints to wear at all times and suggested that I needed to stay on the ibuprofen indefinitely.

My boss, Gregor, noticed the wrist splints the first day I wore them and took me aside for a very short but scarring conversation. He told me that he had seen more than one of his colleagues at Xerox PARC end their careers with an RSI. He then asked if I needed some weeks or months of paid time off.

That was the last thing I wanted to hear. I had finally hit my stride and could not imagine stepping away from the user community that we were delivering for. I was in silent despair and set out to figure out a solution on my own, rather than continuing with the masking effects of ibuprofen. But I also recognized that it was more than a half year into this unresolved problem. I was getting closer to the point of permanent damage that could result from my injury; the very outcome that I was trying to avoid.

I threw away the ibuprofen and began my first experiment: I borrowed different input devices to see if they would make a difference. I used various mice, trackballs, and split keyboards that were fairly common among the staff who worked into the later hours. Nothing other than time away from the keyboard made much of a difference. The less I coded, the better it got. I felt completely stuck, as I could not imagine doing anything else but code.

I tried to narrow down the problem. Starting with a fresh day, it took about six hours for the soreness to get to the point where I was forced to stop. And while my left hand would have some pain and was treated the same way by the nurse, it really was my right hand—the mouse hand—causing the debilitation. My next experiment was simple; learn to use my left hand to mouse and have twice the capacity for coding in the day. However, the purchase request for a left-handed mouse came back with a request to return my first mouse. After some explanation, I got the second mouse and a very unproductive two weeks followed of forcing myself to use the mouse with my left hand. This provided the runway I needed to explore further.

While I had a temporary solution, I felt there was something fundamentally wrong with mouse clicks becoming my personal productivity bottleneck. I then noticed that Douglas Englebart was going to present at PARC Forum, our regular lecture series. Englebart, a former employee, took us through the backstory of the "mother of all demos," a timely presentation of his new invention of "computer mouse" that augmented his use of the keyboard. That caused me to reflect on how I was using the mouse while coding. It did not seem to align to what Englebart had originally envisioned.

While programming, productivity should involve typing lines of code. What I loved most about my job was writing that code, and I was good at cutting out extraneous and distracting activities outside of it. So why on earth was I using the mouse so much when my hands should have been spending most of their time on the keys?

My resentment of every mouse click grew as this continued to be the bottleneck for the hours I could spend coding before the RSI would relapse. A year later, while starting my PhD, I finally had the time to do a more principled examination of where those wasteful mouse clicks were going. To better understand this ground truth of my own coding activity, I created an extension to the popular Eclipse IDE (integrated development environment) that would automatically track all of my activity while I was coding.

My first realization from this initial Gemba walk over my activity history was that, while most of my keystrokes went into writing code, more than half of my interactions while coding were related to clicking around to look for the information I needed to write that code. The majority of these interactions went into clicking through folders and tree-type views, as well as repeated searches and clicks on results.

I ran my ideas by my supervisor, Gail Murphy, and built a visualization. Then something interesting happened. It turned out that, for the most part, I was accessing parts of the code that I had accessed before— searching and clicking around on the same artifacts over and over again. This was very surprising to me, as I had assumed I was finding new information most of the time. But the data showed the opposite. There was something very wrong about this.

The whole point of software architecture is to make it easy to localize code changes. Bad architectures mean that when adding a new feature or defect fix, the developer needs to make changes in many places across the code for what should have been a localized addition. Ironically, my team at PARC was working on an aspect-oriented programming language to localize crosscutting changes; yet it did not seem to be helping me. There was a deeper mismatch between the work that was arriving in my backlog and the architecture, and it was no longer clear to me that better programming languages would ever solve it.

To get a better sense of the intersection between the incoming work and my activity coding, I expanded my monitoring tool to track every interaction I had with the computer. I experimented further by using this interaction-determined context view as my main navigation tool. My mouse clicks dropped so substantially that my arms felt the difference within a couple of weeks. At that point, I knew that I was onto a substantial discovery. Gail recognized my excitement and helped me define a real experiment before getting carried away further.

Six months later, I had the software, the study design, and the ethics approval to run the same experiment I had run on myself on six professional developers working at the IBM software development facility in Toronto. My initial intention was solely data collection, but then Gail convinced me to get a more qualitative sense of the participants by visiting the site and conducting in-depth interviews with each of them face to face.

In doing the study, the participants got their first glimpse of what it was like to have the context of their work connected automatically (something that developers at that time had not seen before), but they all had the same complaint: as soon as they switched tasks, all of the relevant code was no longer relevant. I had them list out the source of their multitasking during the interviews. Every one of those context switches related to some communication that had come in for them to move to a more urgent feature, defect, or security fix. Once that was done, they would move to a technical debt reduction or new API they were working on, only to be interrupted again and again.

The day I concluded the interviews, I stayed awake the entire night, processing what I had learned, then the first epiphany dawned on me. It was possible to capture and connect the context of coding, but the real challenge—the one that caused my RSI—was not about the code; it was about the disconnect between the coding activity, which was a function of the software architecture, and the work flowing through the value stream. That was the biggest bottleneck on these developers' productivity; and I realized that, at a smaller scale, this was exactly what was happening to me. But the problem was much worse at the scale that these professional developers were working, due to how much was flowing through their value stream.

Epiphany 1: Software productivity declines and thrashing increases as software scales, due to disconnects between the architecture and the value stream.

The problem seemed so fundamental that Gail and I started planning a bigger user study in order to achieve a statistically significant research result. Using the growing popularity of my experimental open-source tool intended to solve this problem, Eclipse Mylyn, we recruited ninety-nine professional developers to track multiple months of their daily coding activity and to baseline their productivity when disconnected from the value stream (versus when connected).

With a subset of sixteen developers who generated enough activity, we validated that realigning the daily work of software developers around the value stream, instead of the software architecture, produced a statistically significant productivity increase. Gail and I published the results at the International Symposium on Foundations of Software Engineering in 2005.[4] Ten years later, most development environments now had some kind of support for connecting developers to value stream artifacts, and a follow-up paper received the Most Influential Paper Award at the Modularity 2015 conference.[5] While that finding continues to be useful, we have since learned that it was actually a symptom of a much bigger problem that went far beyond developers.

The Missing Layer: The Second Epiphany

To learn more about the ground truth of enterprise value streams, in 2007, Gail Murphy, Robert Elves, and I spun Tasktop out of the University of British Columbia. With our assumptions based on what software development is like in open-source and tech companies, we were about to find out how flawed our understanding of the realities of enterprise IT were. We landed a large customer, which I'll refer to as FinCo, that wanted to remove duplicate data entry that was happening among thousands of its IT staff. The problem was, at this large a scale, different IDEs were used, and many of the IT staff did not use an IDE at all. The various software delivery specialists lived in testing tools, operations tools, and requirements management and planning tools.

With Rick, our sales leader, Rob and I visited FinCo to walk the shop floor and get a better sense of what our visionary champion was talking about. We sought to understand why on earth it was not a good enough gain to just solve this problem for developers, which should have amounted to most of their software headcount spend. This Gemba walk led me to my second epiphany.

As we were very much in Lean startup mode at the time, we started experimenting with adapting our developer tool to meet the needs of all the other specialists in IT at FinCo. We realized from this that the developer problem we were solving was not limited to developers; it encompassed the way that development needed to connect to operations, quality assurance, and the business. Attempting to solve this with a tool that connected the value stream on the developers' desktop could not solve that problem. Rob then hacked up a prototype for FinCo that flowed information from the developer IDEs across the other tools in the value stream in a peer-to-peer fashion.

Upon examining the architecture of that solution, we realized that the developer problem was only the tip of the iceberg. The real problem at FinCo was that two fundamentally disconnected value streams had countless IT specialists spending a large amount of time each day manually entering information across tools and providing status updates and reports. And in each case, the manual updates were being made in one kind of project-management-and-tracking tool or another.

This layered onto the disconnect we had witnessed between the software architecture and the value streams, but at FinCo that disconnect was even worse. The operational infrastructure and lack of deployment automation and orchestration meant that not only the software architecture but the operational infrastructure were disconnected from the value stream. These observations led me to my second epiphany—that disconnects between the project management model, the end-to-end delivery architecture, and the value stream are the bottleneck to software productivity at scale.

Epiphany 2: Disconnected software value streams are the bottlenecks to software productivity at scale. These value-stream disconnects are caused by the misapplication of the project-management model.

Conclusion

The problems explored in this chapter, the proliferation of repositories and tools, and the lack of an entire infrastructure layer at these organizations led me to my second epiphany—the realization that disconnected software value streams are the number-one bottleneck to software productivity at scale. These disconnects span all software specialists, from business stakeholders to support staff. They are the result of a misalignment between the end-to-end delivery architecture and the project management model with the product-oriented software value streams. Relating back to manufacturing, they are akin to each specialist dumping parts at the next workstation and expecting their colleague to pick them up, count them, and report to the project manager on the result before being able to proceed with any value-adding work. The remaining question is whether these disconnects are fundamental or whether they can be resolved to realign enterprise IT organizations around product-oriented value streams. Before we can answer that question and revisit the third epiphany, we need to examine the evidence of why these disconnects exist in the first place.

Standards.

CHAPTER 8

Specialized Tools and the Value Stream

The user studies and experiences around the first two epiphanies made it clear to me that disconnected tools were causing a crippling fragmentation of the value stream. The fragmentation affected developers on an individual level by dramatically decreasing their productivity. That same fragmentation was having similarly problematic effects at the organization level. For the technologists who have witnessed this firsthand, I can tell you that these bottlenecks in development and in operations are all related to this problem.

The question becomes, what is the solution? Can we put everything into a single repository? This worked early in this Installation Period, when many organizations worked entirely in a tool network provided by Rational; and it is similar to the approach taken by tech giants and popular open-source forges, including Apache and Eclipse. But is it feasible and desirable for other organizations to pursue this approach? Or is there something more fundamental happening, given the sheer level of Agile and DevOps tool network complexity that we see in the market today? Can new tools that provide a single pane of glass across repositories solve this problem, as Mylyn has historically and Slack has more recently? Or is there a more fundamental infrastructure issue lurking here?

In this chapter, we will cover the cause of the tool proliferation that we've seen with the DevOps and Agile tool landscape. We'll discuss the nature and result of disconnects in our value streams. Finally, we'll study 308 enterprise IT tool networks and review the lessons that will allow us to plan for and create effective Value Stream Networks, regardless of the tools that are used.

Specialization to Generalization
and Back Again

At the Leipzig plant, the 1- and 2-Series line is composed of the software equivalent of hundreds of different tools and processes. I presented at BMW's internal vendor conference a year ago, and now I recognize the logos of the industrial technology companies that exhibited there; they are visible at the various workstations of the production line. While the individual stations are fascinating to watch, it is the synchronized coordination of these various steps and vendor-supplied machines that is so impressive.

"You see how the focus is on the flow," Rene says. "This is how we need software production to work. We experiment with many specialized tools and systems, and as you have seen, they are different on the different lines. But we always start with the flow and make sure that the tools support the flow."

"I recently visited the Rolls-Royce plant," Rene continues. "Due to the craftsmanship put into each step, their takt time is two hours, and they take pride in the many manual steps. Even more interesting was the experience that I had with the BMW Z Series many years ago. You would think of the Z Series as fitting into your 'Incubation Zone,' as they were not intended for mass production. The amazing thing about that was that a single team of about one hundred people managed the entire value stream of the car— so, similar to the i8, but all production was done by one team. It was similar to the 'feature teams' that we have been talking about. The team even did support for the car."

"What do you mean support for the car?" I interject. I had been following Rene's point on the crossfunctional team up to this point.

"If there was a maintenance issue with this car," Rene says, "the same team that built the car would fix the problem. How is that for Dev taking responsibility for Ops? It was an interesting experiment that we learned a lot from. But as you can see, the more we scale production, the more we need to specialize people, processes, and tools. But we can still incorporate the learnings of the feature team experiences at this scale."

Functional Specialization and Tool Proliferation

Software delivery has become too complex for one tool, one team, or even one organization. The shocking waste in developers' days, the ways we have seen that cascade across IT specialists, and the proliferation of specialized tools stem from the same problem. Something has changed with the growing division of labor in IT, and that has resulted in the specialization of the various IT staff's tools.

The FinCo experience opened my eyes to how many tools and specialists were involved in large-scale software delivery. But why was FinCo unable to get everything into a single issue tracker, like we had done at the Eclipse Foundation? To this day, Eclipse is continuing to track hundreds of thousands of work items across sixty million lines of code in a single issue tracker, source repository, and continuous-delivery system.[1] It is tempting to dismiss all of those needs as a function of legacy product and IT portfolios, but it would be a mistake to dismiss the different needs of specialists, ranging from product managers to requirements managers, to business analysts, team leads, developers, testers, performance specialists, operations staff, and support staff. The different specialized areas we identified in studying the 308 toolchains are visible in Figure 8.1.

In some cases, different lines of business at FinCo had different tools. For example, the developers building Java apps were using Agile issue trackers different from those building Microsoft .NET apps, as each was tailored for that particular platform. However, in aggregate, the proliferation of tools we were finding in every enterprise IT organization was more surprising than I had ever expected; and some of it was indeed due to legacy tools proliferating. But the complexity that we were working on with FinCo was more fundamental.

As software development has scaled, the various practitioner roles have sought tools specialized for their jobs. A tool that's designed for tracking customer tickets is very different from one used for tracking issues on an Agile backlog, or another that's targeted to business analysts modeling customer-use cases and workflows. Even so, the tools may appear nearly identical in terms of their underlying data models, work flow models, and collaboration tracking facilities. This is why smaller organizations are able to use a single developer-centric issue tracker. However, as the complexity of the work is scaled, so is the pressure on the tools to specialize.

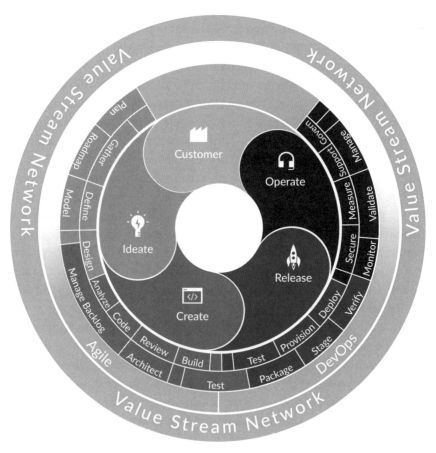

Figure 8.1: Agile and DevOps Tool Roles and Specialization

Modern software specialists have demanded user experiences and systems of engagement tailored for their particular roles. This has put pressure on vendors to specialize, and the current influx in variants of tools can be likened to a Cambrian explosion of the tool network, with hundreds of Agile and DevOps tools available on the market today.

From the study of the 308 tool networks, we have been able to extract two kinds of complexity in enterprise IT tool networks:

- **Fundamental complexity:** This includes all heterogeneity that improves the flow of business value by supporting the needs of specialized stakeholders. For example, based on our data, an organization developing a Java application is more likely to use Atlassian Jira, while those developing .NET and Azure apps are more likely to use Microsoft VSTS.
- **Accidental complexity:** This includes all of the heterogeneity in the tool stack that does not improve the flow of business value. Tools inherited as a result of mergers and acquisitions, or independent selection of similarly functioned tools due to a lack of centralized governance, fall into this category. For example, an organization could have three bug trackers: (1) a twenty-year-old legacy tool created in-house, (2) a new developer-favored issue tracker, and (3) an open-source issue tracker that resulted from an acquisition.

From a value stream architecture point of view, both types of complexity must be accounted for. Reducing the accidental complexity of tools should be an ongoing effort, as this is a form of value stream debt. As with any production line, for each fundamentally different type of work, there should only be, at most, one tool in the value stream providing the support for that function. What's more problematic is when organizations cannot distinguish between accidental complexity and fundamental complexity. Examining the value streams, we have identified the following instances for fundamental complexity:

- **Stakeholder specialization:** The various stakeholders of software delivery require different tools in order to be effective at their particular discipline. Support people need tools that support service-level agreements (SLAs) or the ITIL process, whereas developers need tools streamlined for a code review and commit process.

- **Scale specialization:** Some tools are specialized to organizational size. For example, a lightweight kanban tool can be great for streamlining the flow of a dozen teams, but a hierarchical requirements tool is necessary for tracking the industry standard requirements of safety-critical systems across work done by thousands of engineers.
- **Platform specialization:** Vendors who provide a development platform often provide a tool-based on-ramp to that platform. For instance, Microsoft provides end-to-end DevOps and Agile tools that are optimized around its Azure offering as the deployment platform, while other vendors specialize on the Java ecosystem.
- **Zone specialization:** A more experimental Incubation Zone product may only require the most lightweight tracking tools that minimize process overhead. More mature products like those in the Performance Zone may require closer integration with business requirements and planning, as well as governance, risk, and compliance tools.
- **Legacy:** The cost and disruption of moving away from a legacy system such as an older tool or in-house defect tracker can be overly high, especially for established products in maintenance or in the Productivity Zone. These can be another source of complexity if modernizing them is not a business priority.
- **Supplier diversity:** As the outsourcing and consumption of open-source software increases, it becomes impractical to expect software suppliers to use the same tools as the sourcing organization. For example, open-source projects tend to use open-source tools, while small suppliers tend to use lightweight tool trackers in place of the enterprise tools needed for large-scale software delivery. This also applies to consulting scenarios in which value streams need to be connected across organizational boundaries.

While the goal of any organization should be to take out the accidental complexity and standardize as much as possible, there is another factor that results in the need for specialization. This is the scale at which an organization functions. We may think of scale as a simple function of company size; however, through the 308 tool networks study and, in particular, the discussions with the organizations on the business drivers that lead to tools and artifact flows, more specific dimensions of scale emerged. These include the numbers of features, products, partners, markets, and platforms that are being served, as summarized in Table 8.1.

Dimension	Description	Example
Features	The more demanding the application domain, the more complex the feature set and the larger the number of specialists and specialized tools there may need to be.	A car infotainment system is fundamentally more complex in terms of features than an entire streaming service UI such as Netflix, as it contains both media playback and car functions.
Products	The number of products an organization needs to support, both internal and external.	Startups may have a small number of external products and no internal products. A large IT organization may have hundreds or thousands of each.
Partners	The more business partners exist, whether within lines of business or external, the more complex the resulting set of value streams.	Partners may require use of their own specialists or tools, and those need to be connected to the overall delivery process.
Markets	Each market or market segment can require a new edition or configuration of the software, increasing complexity.	If an organization sells both business-to-consumer and business-to-business, it may need two separate support channels connected to multiple value streams.
Platforms	Development and cloud platforms tend to be tightly coupled to delivery tools and require or encourage use of those tools.	Choosing Microsoft Azure as a hosting platform adds the corresponding tools to the tool chain, as the Java ecosystem tools tend not to be tailored for Azure.

Table 8.1: Dimensions of Scale

Some of the organizations that were early arrivals to the Age of Software have created businesses that thrive by focusing on a highly simplified product offering that limits complexity along these dimensions. Twitter and Netflix are great examples of this. Instead of investing in complexity in the feature or product dimensions, they created streamlined user experiences and applied focus to creating infrastructures that could host these relatively simple products at internet scale.

In general, reducing any accidental complexity along these dimensions can help substantially by making the resulting software easier to manage and evolve. However, for many organizations, complexity is a fundamental part of the business. Though reducing it should be a continual effort, we need a way to understand and manage it in those cases.

The reason for this is fundamental. Software delivery is one of the most complex endeavors undertaken by humanity. That means a growing amount of functional specialization is necessary due to the sheer amount of expertise required, as evidenced by other disciplines in previous ages. The result, not unlike what we have seen in advanced manufacturing, is that a large and diverse vendor ecosystem has been creating a growing number of specialized tools to support the growing tool network complexity. But specialized tools are not new. For example, we have numerous tools for email and for working with files, and they interoperate well using standard protocols and data formats. So why were we seeing all the evidence of non-value-added work?

Seeing the Disconnects in the Value Stream

Across user studies and summarized throughout this book, I've seen symptoms of thrashing—in particular, in the parts of the tool network that store flow items. It is this layer of the tool network that defines how work flows between the people and the teams that define the value stream. This layer is as close as we come to the hand-offs that happen on a car production line; except, in many cases, there is no production line, just a focus on deploying tools to particular workstations. The developers and other specialists are doing all of the hand-offs manually or are ignoring the hand-offs. For example, by asking that a support person log into their tool to get more detail on a defect fix (or vice-versa), the support person tells the developers that they need to get more detail on what to fix from the support desk tool (Figure 8.2). The treatment of risks is particularly disconcerting. At FinCo, developers obtained a spreadsheet of security vulnerabilities from a downstream tool. Then they needed to manually enter those into their issue tracker and do additional error-prone manual triage and prioritization.

In addition, work that should flow to completion often does not because it routinely gets lost, resulting in delays and rework. When an automotive software supplier we studied started measuring the root causes of rework and delay work, they noticed that up to 20% of requirements and defects were either lost or contained errors due to manual hand-offs. After they connected the Value Stream Network between them and the automotive OEM (original equipment manufacturer) for defect and requirement exchange, that rate dropped to below 0.1%. But before that, the manual process was akin to dropping off a bucket of parts at their workstation, leaving, and expecting the developers to sort through all of them as new parts were being dropped onto the pile.

MoPS

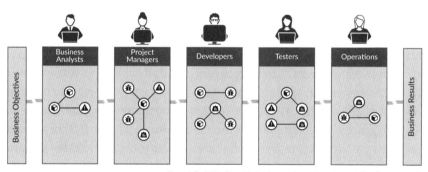

Figure 8.2: Fragmented Value Streams - *Working Together!!*

Mining the Ground Truth of Enterprise Tool Networks

Inspired in part by the visit to the BMW Group plant, where the ground truth was always visible by walking the production line, I wanted to gather as much data as possible about what these 308 organizations' "factory floors" really looked like. The key thing that we learned from previous studies is that tool repositories are the ground truth. In other words, they are the most directly observable information that defines software delivery.

The challenge is getting access to that tool-repository data. To date, much of the data that has informed Agile and DevOps transformations comes from surveys. Survey data is useful for collecting a holistic and period view of the value stream; however, to see the ground truth, we need the system data that provides a continuous and comprehensive view of the flow of work, as summarized in the *ACM Queue* article "DevOps Metrics: Your Biggest Mistake Might Be Collecting the Wrong Data."[2] The issue is the end-to-end system data is hidden behind an organization's firewall or locked in private tool repositories. Some vendors may have access to a segment of the value stream—for example, a software-as-a-service support-desk tool vendor might have cross-company information on support tickets; however, that slice misses all of the upstream data from development, design, and business analysis.

While working with Fortune Global 500 organizations undergoing transformations, solutions architects from Tasktop create a "Value Stream Integration" diagram with the IT administrators of each tool to plan a deployment. These diagrams contain the repositories, artifact types stored in those repositories, and, most important, the data on how those artifact types are related in terms of value stream flow. The diagrams, an example of which is shown in Figure 8.3, capture a moment-in-time summary of what each of the tools in the value stream is, what each of the key artifacts is, and how these artifacts are connected—or in some cases, how they *should be* connected. Note that these diagrams were not collected through an academic study but through a data collection process put in place for working with the enterprise IT tool administrators and their tools.

Of the thirty-eight organizations, 28% were in the Fortune Global 500 and from a broad range of industries, from financial services to transportation. (The full summary and analysis from 2017 study is summarized in the *IEEE Software* article "Mining the Ground Truth of Enterprise Toolchains.")[3] Here, I will review only the key findings needed for us to understand how to create effective Value Stream Networks (Chapter 9) in our organizations.

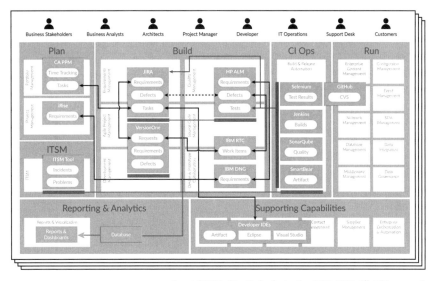

Figure 8.3: Value Stream Integration Diagrams

Altogether, the organizations reported using fifty-five different tools to support their software delivery value streams. This figure itself is surprising, as these organizations reported that a decade ago the same information was kept in one or two tools provided by IBM Rational and HP. Table 8.2 indicates which types of tools are used today, and we can see that Agile and ALM tools dominate, as expected, but that IT service management, project and portfolio management, and requirements management also form a key part of the tool network. Connecting customer relationship management (CRM) and security tools is still rare, but some organizations are already considering these as part of their software value stream.

Another important finding is the distribution of artifacts corresponding to flow items across the tools. While tool selection varied greatly, there was more commonality with artifacts. For example, "defect" was the most commonly used artifact, followed by "requirement" and "user story." The key finding was that each of the two dozen artifact types that we studied spanned numerous tools. It was from these artifacts that we extracted the more generic flow items.

Type of Tool	Tool Usages Reported
Agile Planning	194
Application life cycle management	259
Change or workflow management	9
Content management	9
Enterprise modeling	1
Issue tracker	8
IT service management	133
Project portfolio management	77
Requirements management	79
Sales	1
Security	2
Test management	28

Table 8.2: Types of Tools Used

Across the 308 organizations, 1.3% used a single tool while 69.3% had artifacts that needed to flow across three or more tools. The most surprising finding was that over 42% of the organizations had four or more tools, indicating the level of specialization in enterprise tool networks. Within these organizations, heterogeneous Agile and DevOps tool networks are the norm. The set of tools used to support the value stream is highly specialized and diverse, while the artifacts that underpin the value stream are consistent and common.

Why Heterogeneous Tools Are Here to Stay

What the 308 tool network study showed is that instead of tool consolidation, we are continuing to see an ongoing wave of specialization and Deployment Period–style "frenzy" as the various specialized functions of software delivery become better defined. For example, the requirements management discipline once contained tools that focused on scale specialization—some vendors created lighter-weight requirements management for smaller systems, with heavy weight, hierarchical, and versioned requirements management for more complex systems. However, requirements management practices vary between pure software systems, such as mobile applications; safety-critical systems, such as medical devices; highly regulated systems, such as banking software; and mixed software/hardware systems, such as airplanes.

Through the Turning Point, the industry trend has been for vendors to provide increasingly specialized tools, similar to how we witnessed the specialization of manufacturing tools in the previous age. Additional specialization is likely to continue in the Deployment Period. For example, Carlota Perez's model predicts that regulations specific to the new technological revolution appear at the start of the Deployment Period.[4] We are already seeing the start of this with new regulations, such as GDPR, and we are seeing increased investment in key areas in support of this, such as information security.[5] This is likely to result in tools further specialized for managing risk and regulation in software value streams. In addition, as the need for product-oriented management grows within the majority of software-driven organizations, another breed of tools will come to support it.

Another key finding from the 308 tool networks study is just how long the older tools remained a key part of the organization's value streams. While it is relatively easy to move between source-code management and continuous-delivery tools, moving between Agile and issue tracking tools is notoriously difficult, as those tools become closely tied to the organization's processes. This means that tools tend to remain in use for the duration of the project or product. Consider one of the oldest tools in the data set—IBM Rational DOORS (Dynamic Object-Oriented Requirements System)—created in the 1980s. Many of today's aircraft, cars, and other highly complex devices continue to track hardware and software requirements in DOORS. If we think back to the Boeing Dreamliner story in Chapter 2, the software requirements for an airplane need to be maintained for approximately sixty years. This implies that tools like DOORS are likely to outlive the current generation of IT professionals.

Is this use of tools provided by a diverse set of suppliers and open-source projects common across the industry or particular to the

Fortune Global 500 organizations studied? We have encountered two notable exceptions. One is startups and small organizations, who do not have the scale discussed above and use fewer tools. The other is the tech giants who have created their own tool networks. For example, Google's value stream artifacts are maintained in an in-house tool that uses the same infrastructure that it uses for its web services.[6] Likewise, Microsoft has created its own internal tool network specific to its own products and value streams; but unlike the other tech giants, Microsoft sells a significant portion of the tool network to its customer base in the form of VSTS (Visual Studio Team Service), TFS (Team Foundation Server), and associated tools. The problem: Microsoft is able to standardize all of its highly complex and successful product delivery on this tool network, but its customer base cannot. For example, 79% of TFS customers also use another tool in that same category, such as Atlassian Jira.[7] The reason is that VSTS grew out of the Microsoft development platforms, but as discussed earlier in this chapter, the prevalence of other platforms has spawned tools from other vendors.

Investments made by tech giants in their internal software delivery platforms are enormous. The internal tool networks directly connect the value streams of software delivery to their business and, as such, provide a tremendous competitive differentiator for these organizations. The 3,500 developers dedicated to Microsoft's developer tools I mentioned at the beginning of Part III should cost in the neighborhood of half a billion dollars annually. Most other tech giants are in a similar ballpark. While a small portion of this flows into tools and open-source projects that other organizations can leverage, overall it creates a barrier for those wanting to compete with the tech giants. Other larger-scale organizations, who are already finding it challenging to compete with the tech giants on talent for building business applications, are left scrambling to assemble tool networks from offerings provided by dedicated tool vendors and open-source solutions.

While this explosion of tools has helped create a very active market, without an infrastructure layer to connect them, the results have been a fraction of the software delivery effectiveness experienced by the tech giants. Attempting to create in-house tools and integrations is a risky and failure-prone approach due to the costs and time frames associated with creating these tools, which then compete internally for budget and talent with the business applications that usually take priority.

So, what is the experience at startups and smaller organizations? While definitive data on this is hard to find, in my personal experience working with startups, the problem is dramatically easier when there are less than one hundred software delivery staff. With the dimensions of scale (Table 8.1) being so much smaller, and the number of staff and processes much smaller as well, startups can support a good portion of their growth in a simplified tool network with one central tool. This makes it easier to connect software delivery to a much simpler set of business management systems. This in turn allows startups to innovate at the speed needed to disrupt incumbents by leveraging highly focused digital products. But the heterogeneity returns once those startups scale and become public companies. To see the golden age in the Deployment Period that Perez's model predicts, we need an infrastructure for innovation that will allow both existing and new enterprises to compete with the software delivery capabilities of the tech giants.

Conclusion

The specialization of software delivery tools is as fundamental as the specializations we witnessed in the previous surges of development. As the new means of production matures, the specialization of roles becomes clearer, as does the need to provide specialists with tools tailored to their roles.

History presents us with the right ways and the wrong ways of handling specialization. Consider the sheer number of doctors and medical professionals that we interact with in a flow through the medical system. Three centuries ago, it would have been a simple flow with a single doctor. However, life expectancy in seventeenth century England was approximately thirty-five years, and it was during the Industrial Revolution that it started rising dramatically.[8] Modern medicine, which has extended life expectancy over the eighty-year mark in some countries, came from a growing sophistication in the understanding of the human body. The only way for humans to master that kind of complexity is with a radical specialization of roles and disciplines. The Association of American Medical Colleges now lists over 120 specializations and subspecialties, each with its own systems and tools.[9] While this specialization has resulted in growing progress, the resulting fragmentation of the knowledge flow is now becoming a bottleneck on the effectiveness of medical practice.

In *Team of Teams: New Rules of Engagement for a Complex World*, General Stanley McChrystal relates that the problem of specialization in the medical disciplines is that it causes disconnects on the "fault lines" between the different teams and specializations of medical practitioners.[10] The lack of a reliable and automated way for information to flow across a patient's history of treatment results in medical errors. A 2016 study published in *John Hopkins Medicine* found that medical errors in the United States are to blame for over 250,000 deaths per year, making those errors the third-leading cause of death in the country.[11]

Specialization allows us to handle ever-growing complexity, but the benefits of specialization can only be fully realized if the silos that it creates can be connected effectively. Some of those silos rely on human collaboration and interaction, as is the topic of General McChrystal's book. But others require an infrastructure and cross-silo integration to give those same people and teams a chance to collaborate and exchange the highly complex knowledge that they process in their daily work.

Once again, we can turn to the Age of Mass Production for guidance and inspiration. The BMW Group Leipzig plant demonstrated no lack of complexity or heterogeneity, with 12,000 suppliers providing the hardware and software that make up the plant's toolchain.[12] Yet every flow is meticulously automated, optimized, and made visible to handle the complexity related to that particular production line. Given that the software that drives our organizations' success is headed to a similar or greater scale of complexity, how can we connect our value streams in a way that gets our organizations on the path that the BMW Group mastered when it learned to produce cars at scale during the last Turning Point?

CHAPTER 9

Value Stream Management

n Chapters 7 and 8, we learned that enterprise IT tool networks are fundamentally heterogeneous and that tool complexity will continue along with the increasing specialization of roles in software delivery that the Deployment Period will bring. The study of 308 tool networks shows us what flows across these various tools. The question now is how we connect all of these tools and artifacts in order to achieve the kind of flow and feedback that I witnessed on the BMW Group's production lines.

Given that the BMW Group has solved this problem for an even larger diversity of suppliers, we should be able to do the same for our software value streams. We should be able to see the bottlenecks in the flow of business value as clearly as the BMW Group can see and manage the bottlenecks in the flow of car production. But how do we do it? Can we simply emulate what was learned in the Age of Mass Production and create our own software production lines? As we will learn in this chapter, the answer is no. Software is fundamentally different, and attempting to directly emulate a model that worked for physical production is the wrong approach. My failed attempts at overapplying manufacturing analogies to software are the root of my third epiphany.

In this chapter, we will cover what it means to search for bottlenecks in a software value stream. We'll discuss the pitfalls of modeling software delivery on mass production and determine that we need to model software value streams as a network. We will then go through the three layers needed to transition an organization from project to product, starting with the tool network, then the artifact, and finally, the Value Stream Network. The chapter will conclude with the three models needed to connect the Value Stream Network to business outcomes, including the Integration Model, the Activity Model, and the Product Model.

Whereas the focus of our discussion so far has been on why shifting from project to product is so urgent and what the resulting management framework looks like, this last chapter of the book will dive into the infrastructure needed to achieve this transition, including a minimal amount of technical detail on the new concept of Value Stream Networks and how to create and manage them.

BMW TRIP Coffee Break at the Bottleneck

Once we leave the production-line buildings and return to the Central Building, we walk past a field of desks and dual monitors and toward the very large cafeteria that we passed on the way in. My feet are starting to feel sore, and I reactively click the ring feature on my watch, which shows me that we have walked almost ten kilometers (a little over six miles) along the lines that day.

"There it is," says Frank, pointing up. "To be specific, this is where we have to batch up the cars leaving the bottleneck. You see, this is the one place in the plant where we have to put the cars out of sequence of orders and then re-sort them later. Can you guess yet what the bottleneck is?"

I cannot. As it is now morning in Pacific time, I am beginning to text Gene Kim the riddle of the plant bottleneck. I feel like I am living a part of *The Phoenix Project* in this moment, and amusingly, neither Gene nor I can come up with the answer with the deliberately limited information Frank has provided.

"The bottleneck is the paint shop. It takes time for the paint to cure, even though we put 70,000 volts of electricity through the car bodies to speed up the process. It also takes time to switch the paint color on the robots that do the spraying. Since it's not currently possible to do all of that in the seventy-second takt time, we need to take the cars out of the just-in-sequence order and sort them into color order for painting. That minimizes the switch-over time. But it also means that the cars need to get sorted out of sequence, then batched up just past the cafeteria, then re-sorted into order sequence. This is the only place in the production line where we have to batch and inventory the cars. And we have made the sorting and re-sorting visible for all staff to see, right above the cafeteria."

This explains the four separate conveyor lines of cars that move above the cafeteria: two toward the batch storage, two back out. Surely the BMW Group has reached a new height of making production work visible. All I can think about is, how can we do the same for IT? I keep trying to connect these two concepts when Rene's voice snaps me out of it.

"Frank," Rene says. "Can we go to the last activity now?"

Frank does not answer but sends off a text message. We finish our coffees.

"Yes," Frank says. "The cars are ready."

It takes me a moment to realize what they are talking about. I had completely forgotten about the test drive that Rene had teased when telling me about the plant visit. We walk back through the plant and out one of the doors near the i-Series building. Outside, a brand new M2, 5 Series, i3, and i8 are parked, with two people standing next to them.

"You will need to be accompanied by a co-pilot," Frank says. "Rene and I can act as two co-pilots; and our colleagues here—both are engineers who work on final integration testing—will also join us."

"Pick a car," Rene says with a smile.

I open the perfectly balanced butterfly doors of the i8 and get in to experience firsthand some of the magnificent business outcomes that the BMW Group delivers.

Looking for Bottlenecks: The Third Epiphany

In the weeks after I left the BMW Group Leipzig plant, I became obsessed with figuring out how we could apply what I had witnessed to software delivery. The key concepts of flow and visibility seemed to translate directly. However, in trying to model out a production-style flow of software delivery, I kept getting stuck. The continuous integration and continuous delivery portions were easy enough to map onto the manufacturing concepts, as they involved a series of automation steps. The "where is the bottleneck" test was easy to apply. If there was any lack of test automation, build automation, or release automation, that instantly became the bottleneck.

However, the dynamics of teams that designed, coded, and shipped features stumped me. In all my time leading software teams who already had the deployment automation in place, I had never experienced the kind of bottleneck that appeared in the manufacturing line. I had experienced plenty of problems with flow, ranging from multiple development teams being blocked by a UX team with insufficient bandwidth, to teams waiting on customer-environment information from support, to numerous teams waiting on APIs to get added to unblock downstream work.

However, none of these issues stopped a release from happening in the same way that a manufacturing-line bottleneck can bring production to a crawl. The graphic designer constraint would result in the team proceeding with help from another team who had a developer with Photoshop skills. The customer-environment bottleneck got the test environment team to create new automations for simulating customer data. And the API dependency resulted in a team creating their own APIs and contributing them to the upstream component when it was time to address that technical debt. In other words, each time a bottleneck appeared, there was a rerouting of the work around the constraint rather than production stopping. The teams would come up with that rerouting to creatively deal with the constraint that had been imposed upon them. There might be a *slowing* of productivity due to the constraint, but each time, the teams were able to reroute the work in a way that ensured flow.

As I was struggling with this problem, Nicole Bryan, Tasktop's VP of Product Management, and Rob Elves (one of Tasktop's co-founders) were working on a seemingly unrelated problem—a visualization of how all of our internal delivery artifacts flowed through our value streams. I had been pushing for manufacturing metaphors that resembled production lines or Value Stream Mapping diagrams when providing feedback on their work. After struggling to implement such views, Nicole became convinced that we were chasing the wrong metaphor. What she and Rob were seeing in our and our customers' value streams were not linear manufacturing processes. The structure they were seeing emerge from the data was much more similar to that of an airline network than a manufacturing line (Figure 9.1).

And that was it—the last piece of the puzzle and the third epiphany, handed to me by Nicole, who had spent the most time looking over the ground truth of the 308 tool networks that we had studied.

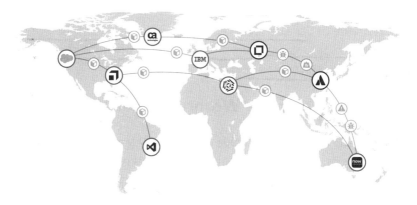

Figure 9.1: More Like an Airline Network

There was some irony, as Rob pointed out, that this epiphany paralleled what Reinertsen had previously proposed about applying principles of computer networks to product development.[1] Did the entire problem stem from the fact that the DevOps community, myself included, was so focused on applying the lessons of Lean manufacturing that we neglected to incorporate Lean product development? Perhaps. However, there was also something fundamentally different going on here, since in software delivery the product development and manufacturing processes are one. This is why reducing the software delivery process to a manufacturing line was so compelling but also wrong.

The process of identifying flow constraints in a linear, batch-based flow differs greatly from optimizing a network's flow. In network management, bottlenecks are constraints that you simply reroute around. The flow does not need to stop as it does in a linear process. For example, if bad weather hits one part of the continent, the air-traffic management system reroutes aircraft so that passengers can get to their destination, though perhaps with some delay. This was directly analogous to what I witnessed working with delivery teams who implemented creative work-arounds to reroute when they encountered bottlenecks. This kind of nearly instantaneous rerouting and retooling is something that a manufacturing line simply cannot do.

> *Epiphany 3: Software value streams are not linear manufacturing processes but complex collaboration networks that need to be aligned to products.*

Pitfalls of the Wrong Mental Model

Engineers and technologists solve complex problems by reducing them to simpler ones. But consider some of the missteps we've taken in past attempts to improve large-scale software delivery. Waterfall development looked great in theory because it made linear the complexity of connecting all the stakeholders in software delivery. But, it failed in practice, as Tommy Mouser and Gary Gruver illustrate in their book *Leading the Transformation: Applying Agile and DevOps Principles at Scale.*[2] Agile development came to the rescue but oversimplified its view of delivery to exclude upstream and downstream stakeholders, such as business analysts and operations staff. DevOps addressed this exclusion by embracing operations, automation, and repeatability of deployment processes. But by overfocusing on linear processes rather than end-to-end flow and feedback, organizations are repeating mistakes by adopting an overly narrow and overly linear view of DevOps.

The ability to stamp out frequent releases in an automated, repeatable way can be a great starting point for DevOps transformations.

But that's only a small step in optimizing a product's end-to-end value stream. The theory of constraints tells us that investing in just one segment of the value stream will not produce results unless that segment is the bottleneck.[3] But how do we know it is the bottleneck? Even more important, what if we're looking for a linear bottleneck in a nonlinear process? For example, in a linear bottleneck a single dependency can become a constraint. But in a network, there may be a path around the dependency. Software teams can be observed taking these alternate paths all the time (e.g., coding around the lack of an API they expected from an upstream team).

Software development comprises a set of manufacturing-like processes. Taken in isolation, each can be thought of as batch flow in which automation and repeatability determine success. For example, in the 1970s, we mastered software assembly with compilers and systems such as GNU, which provided batch-style repeatability for building very large codebases. In the following decade, code generation became the automation stage we now take for granted when building mobile user interfaces. Today, we're in the process of mastering code deployment, release, and performance management, making frequent releases a reliable and safe process. However, each of these is only a single building block of an end-to-end software value stream, that's analogous to the various stages of robots that form, weld, and assemble a car. But with software, these various stages do not combine to form the simple one-way batch flow of a production line.

If we could take a virtual MRI of the workflows in a large IT organization (similar to viewing a moving X-ray of the BMW Group plant from above), what underlying structure would we see? I've done this for my own organization, and the resulting visualizations look nothing like a production line. But they do bear a fascinating resemblance to the airline network maps at the back of in-flight magazines. If you imagine a visualization of the flow of airplanes over time, adapting to route changes or bottlenecks due to severe weather and delayed crews, you're starting to get the picture.

If we try to map an IT organization to look like an air traffic network, what are the nodes? The routes? How do we map the flows of features and fixes across projects, products, and teams? We will answer these questions in this chapter. All of our learnings from the 308 tool networks indicates that this network-based model is more representative of software development than a linear manufacturing flow. To identify bottlenecks and optimize software delivery, we must first learn how to create and then manage this network.

More Like Routing Airplanes Than Manufacturing Cars

At its core, the end-to-end software life cycle is a business process that delivers value to end users. Many Lean concepts are relevant when we're shifting our thinking of flow from a production line to a network, such as small batch sizes and one-piece flow to minimize work in progress (WIP). However, to avoid overapplying manufacturing analogies—or worse, continuing down the path of the wrong mental model—we must more clearly define the key differences between managing the iterative and network-based value streams of software development, and managing the linear value streams of manufacturing:

- **Variability:** Manufacturing has a fixed, well-defined set of variations for what will emerge from the end of the line, whereas the design of software features is open ended. Manufacturing needs to minimize variability; software development needs to embrace it.
- **Repeatability:** Manufacturing is about maximizing throughput of the *same* widget; software is about maximizing the iteration and feedback loops that continually *reshape* the widget. We need repeatability at each stage of software delivery, such as reliable automated deployment, but each end-to-end process needs to be optimized for flow, feedback, and continual learning, not just repeatability.
- **Design frequency:** Manufactured products like cars are designed up front in project-oriented cycles spanning years. Changes in design are infrequent and require altering the production line itself. With software, the shift to product-oriented features increases the frequency of design to match the rate of

flow items passing through the value stream. The design happens inside, not outside, the production system.

- **Creativity:** Manufacturing processes aim to achieve the highest feasible level of automation, which is facilitated by removing any creative and nondeterministic work from the production process. In contrast, software delivery focuses on enabling creativity and collaboration at each step, using automation to support creativity.

Metcalfe's law tells us that a network's value grows with its connectedness.[4] If our Value Stream Network has insufficient connectedness, is there any point in optimizing any particular stage? For instance, assume that no formalized feedback loop exists between operations and service-desk staff working with an IT service management tool, such as ServiceNow; and developers coding in an Agile tool, such as Jira; and project managers working in a project management tool, such as CA PPM. In this case, will investing millions into continuous delivery produce any measurable business benefit? To answer these questions, we need to be able to measure and visualize the Value Stream Network.

The Leipzig plant's bottleneck was the paint shop. The need to re-sort the cars by the desired color, batch them into a temporary inventory, and reorder them into the just-in-time sequence is the incredible mechanical ballet that takes place above the plant's lunchroom, the ultimate tribute to value stream visibility. As I walked out of the Leipzig plant, my perspective was transformed by the ingenuity, innovation, and managerial sophistication that the BMW Group has attained. It's now time for us to lay down the groundwork and new models that will let us attain this kind of pursuit of perfection for scaling how software is built. As long as we continue viewing software delivery as a linear manufacturing process, we'll remain stuck in the age before flight.

The Value Stream Network

In the Flow Framework, we have identified three layers of abstraction that create the Value Stream Network (Figure 9.2). The goal of these layers is to connect the implementation details of the tool layer to a much more abstract and business value–oriented view provided by Value Stream Metrics.

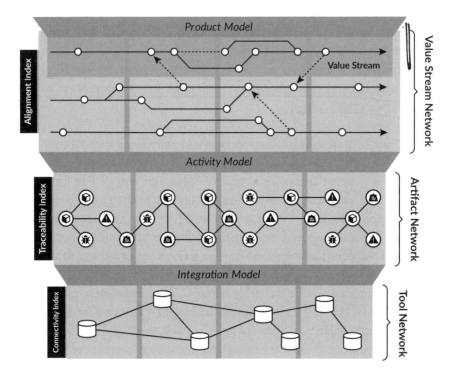

Figure 9.2: Value Stream Network

The bottom-most layer of the Flow Framework is the tool network, within which the nodes are tools and the links between them are lines of cross-tool integrations. This network is defined by the *Integration Model*. Once that is in place, the various artifacts and work items that developers and others create are instantiated within the tool network. When viewed across tools, these form the *artifact network*. The nodes in the artifact network are artifacts, such as "tickets" and "defects," and these nodes are connected by the relationships between these artifacts. From the artifact network, we can create the Value Stream Network and use the *Activity Model* to map the detailed artifacts to the more generic flow items and flow states needed to produce flow metrics. The final model that is needed is the *Product Model*, which aligns the value streams in the Value Stream Network to the product-oriented business results that we want to measure.

Each of these three networks provides a different level of insight into software delivery. For example, measurement of the tool network can determine which tools are the most used and what the usage profile is across the entire organization. The artifact network can be used to systematically measure things like the code-commit-to-code-deploy cycle time for each team. Facilitating these kinds of cross-tool metrics is a benefit of connecting these two network layers. However, the focus of the Flow Framework is to enable the third layer, the Value Stream Network, which is what provides business-level insights into software delivery. The following sections detail the core concepts needed to create, connect, and manage these networks. The end goal of doing this is to enable product-oriented Value Stream Management, which is defined by Christopher Condo and Diego Lo Giudice of Forrester as:

> A combination of people, process, and technology that maps, optimizes, visualizes, and governs business value flow (including epics, stories, work items) through heterogeneous enterprisesoftware delivery pipelines. Value stream management tools are the technology underpinnings of VSM practice.[5]

⟲ Connecting the Tool Network

The tool network (Figure 9.3) will be immediately familiar to those who have managed or procured the tools that support the value stream. This is simply the collection of hosted and on-premise tools that contain the artifacts that support the four flow items. As soon as more than one tool is present, the only way to achieve flow and feedback is by connecting the corresponding tools that the flow items span.

To measure this, the *connectivity index* is a ratio of the tools and artifact containers within those tools that have been integrated to those that have not. For example, if only two of five tools have been connected, and only a portion of project or product areas within those

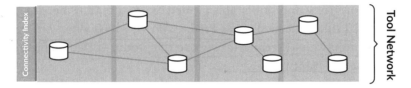

Figure 9.3: The Tool Network

tools integrated, the connectivity index will be low. The connectivity index is the key measure for providing a level of confidence for flow metrics. If the service desk tool has not been connected, the connectivity index will be less than 100%. This will also mean that flow time metrics cannot be accurate for flow items that originate from customer-support cases, as that part of the value stream is not being captured.

Connectivity Index: The ratio of repositories in the tool network that have been connected to those that have not.

For enterprise IT organizations who rely on multiple vendor-provided, in-house, and open-source tools, the disconnects in the tool network layer of the Value Stream Network are what prevent the necessary flow and feedback. As long as a developer tool like Jira is not connected to a service-desk tool like ServiceNow, the corresponding lack of flow and feedback between those two silos creates an information bottleneck. This is where the connectivity index comes into play, as it is a measure of the degree to which information can flow end to end across value streams.

Connecting the Tool Network with the Integration Model

When more than one tool is present in the tool network, the tools must be integrated to support flow. The purpose of integration is to connect the artifacts being worked on to metrics that the Flow Framework measures. This is the critical and often missing link needed to connect business metrics with the ground truth of software delivery. While it is generally easy to get at the raw data from the repositories in the tool network, meaningful business-level reporting, with accurate correlation across tools, is impossible without an Integration Model that connects a cross-tool artifact network.

The Integration Model defines the cross-tool work items and related artifacts that flow through the value streams and allows them to be mapped to the four flow items. Each of these artifacts is stored in one of the tools in the tool network. When attempting to report directly from tool repositories, the sheer volume and variability of artifact types, schemas, and workflow states impedes meaningful reporting and visibility.

In our study, one of the 308 organizations' artifacts supported over 200 workflow states on a single artifact. While this level of detail and complexity can be important to the individual specialists and teams, it is far too fine grained for measuring business value. For example, an internal BI (business intelligence) team may need to put in place a large number of mappings and logic to extract workflow states relevant to the business, only to have those change when a team switches its methodology and alters its workflow model.

This is where the Integration Model comes in (Figure 9.4). It provides a layer of abstraction and insulation that maps the detailed artifact types to the flow items and their associated states. The Integration Model enables easy reporting of flow metrics across any number of tools.

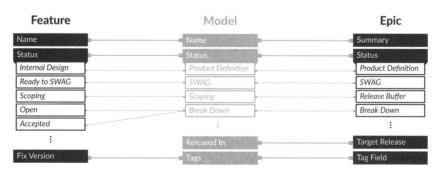

Figure 9.4: Integration Model Field Mapping

In addition to enabling business-level feedback, the Integration Model is key to implementing flow when multiple tools are involved. Different tools specialize in different stages of the delivery pipeline. In this scenario, work item artifacts such as user stories will span one or more tools. A user story could originate in an ideation tool used by a business partner, then be a user story in an Agile planning tool, then be implemented in a developer-centric team tool, then be deployed by a release automation tool, and then have tickets filed that relate to it in a support-desk tool. In this case, artifacts related to the story would have been created in five different tools but would correspond to a single artifact in the more abstract Integration Model.

For large organizations, the effect of connecting the tool network through the Integration Model can itself be transformational. For instance, when an enterprise insurance company connected the tool used by developers with the one used for quality management, they witnessed a 22% increase in the employee-engagement surveys for the corresponding staff that same quarter.[6] The improvement was attributed to the reduction in duplicate data entry and other related forms of friction that were caused by the disconnects.

Finally, the Integration Model provides the mapping between each of those artifact types and the corresponding flow item. In doing so, it also provides mapping between that artifact's potentially numerous workflow states and the four flow states. (Figure 9.5 depicts a simplified version of the Integration Model in use at Tasktop.)

Depending on the complexity of the tool network and organization, connecting the tool network can be a complex activity. For example, from the 308 tool networks studied, we observed that some organizations will have dozens of different and independently evolved artifact types corresponding to a defect flow item. Ideally, this kind of accidental complexity would be rationalized into a common set of artifact types, but that may not always be feasible in the time frame of the transformation initiative. The Integration Model addresses this by insulating flow metrics from that complexity. Over time, any accidental complexity in the tools' artifact schemas can be simplified to reduce the number of mappings between the tool schemas and the Integration Model.

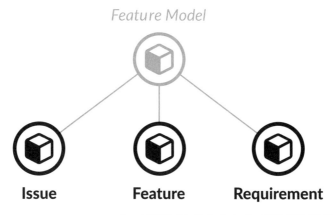

Feature Model

Issue   **Feature**   **Requirement**

Figure 9.5: Integration Model Artifact Mapping

The Integration Model provides a fundamental benefit to the IT teams managing the tool infrastructure. The work of Carliss Baldwin and colleagues at the Harvard Business School has demonstrated that software modularity provides business value by increasing optionality.[7] A key goal of the Integration Model is to add modularity to the tool network. It does so by allowing different tools to be plugged into the value stream, or for tools specific to a product's value stream to be easily onboarded. If there is a need to deploy a new security analysis tool, that tool only needs to be mapped into the Integration Model and not into every other tool and product area in the tool network. Onboarding tools, offboarding tools, and supporting reorganizations becomes much easier through the tool network modularity provided by the Integration Model.

Producing the Artifact Network

The Integration Model defines the routes that business value can flow through in the Value Stream Network. From a software architecture point of view, it is analogous to a type hierarchy of artifacts. The corresponding instances of work items that flow through the Integration Model create the *artifact network*. For example, if an organization has one hundred value streams, this means that a single Integration Model can be instantiated one hundred times into one hundred different artifact flows. It's in the artifact network that all of the work being produced by teams is visible.

In order to ensure end-to-end visibility, the artifact network must ensure every artifact is connected to all other artifacts it is related to. If a new team starts work but uses a methodology that is not connected to the Integration Model, a set of artifacts will appear in the artifact network but will not be mapped to the four flow items. As such, these artifacts will be visible in the artifact network but will not be connected to the flow metrics.

These artifact "islands" are opaque to the business and impede value stream visibility. To address this, the *traceability index* tracks the measure of connected to disconnected artifacts in the artifact network. A low traceability index implies that the disconnected portion of the work is not being tracked by flow metrics and, as such, is not visible to the corresponding stakeholders. The higher the traceability index, the more reliable the input the Flow Framework provides to the business. For full business-level traceability, the target for the index should be 100%.

|| *Traceability Index: The measure of artifact connection breadth and depth relative to artifact type.*

Since the traceability index is based on the mapping of the tool network artifacts to the Integration Model, it also indicates the amount of traceability automation that is present in the Value Stream Network. If there is no automated traceability between a requirement, the corresponding code changes, and test cases, then the resulting disconnected artifacts will result in a lower traceability index. To support governance, regulation, and compliance, the automation of traceability is an integral aspect of a Value Stream Network, and the traceability index reflects the degree of that automation.

The story of the Boeing 787 brake software in Chapter 2 illustrates how critical traceability automation is to evolving and maintaining large-scale software. For the majority of organizations, the need to "version everything" is well understood, as source files that are not under version control cannot be properly managed. Value Stream Networks build on that concept and extend it to "connect everything" that is flowing through the value stream. For instance, at Tasktop we have automated traceability of every single artifact, from the initial customer request (originating in Salesforce), to the many tools involved in creating the feature, to the release that provides the corresponding feature. Reports or audits of value delivered become a simple query of the artifact network.

Finally, in order to categorize the various phases that the artifacts defining the flow items pass through as they are being worked on, the artifact network employs an *Activity Model*. The Activity Model identifies each of the specific activities performed in the value stream and maps those to the concrete workflow states defined by the Integration Model. In addition, it maps these activities to the four flow states, enabling a consistent way of measuring flow across all artifacts.

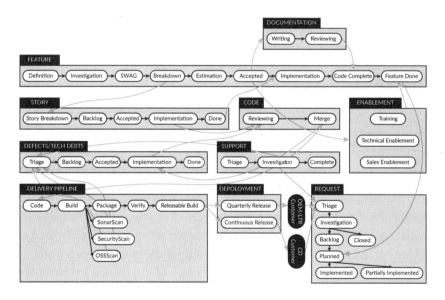

Figure 9.6: Sample Artifacts and Workflow States Corresponding to Activity Mode

The phases themselves are based on an organization's software delivery and business processes. A highly regulated organization may have additional phases related to additional controls, whereas a car manufacturer may have additional phases related to electronic-control-unit integration. Once these phases are specified and mapped, it is possible to see at exactly which stage each artifact is during its life cycle. Figure 9.6 shows a simplified version of Tasktop's internal artifact and workflow states that form the basis of the Activity Model.

Aligning the Value Stream Network with the Product Model

The topmost layer is the Value Stream Network itself. The lower two layers provide the infrastructure for automated flow and feedback that feed this network. These two layers are all that is needed to connect teams and specialists while removing manual work and reporting, but it is this third layer that aligns the work flowing through the tools and teams that the business stakeholders need to see. This layer shows how much business value each value stream is delivering and where its bottlenecks and opportunities may lie.

The *Product Model* addresses the fundamental disconnect that exists between the software architecture and business-level product offerings. What we examined with the 308 tool networks is that the structure of Agile tools is aligned to the hierarchical structure of software components. This structure is often a function of the modularity mechanisms of programming languages or of the legacy structure of the software's evolution.

Discussions with software architects provided us with further insight for this lack of one-to-one alignment between the repositories in the tool network and the product value stream. Technologists tend to create software architectures around technology boundaries instead of value stream boundaries. The result is a lack of alignment between the three key structures involved with software delivery: the organization and team structure, the software architecture, and the value stream architecture. New programing frameworks, modularity mechanisms, and organizational concepts, such as feature teams, show promise in improving this alignment. What the Product Model provides is a mapping between the existing artifact containment structure present in the tool network and the product-oriented value streams that are aligned to business value delivery (Figure 9.7).

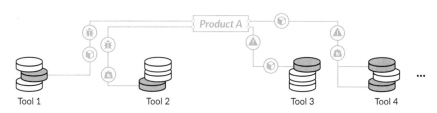

Figure 9.7: The Product Model

The final component of the Flow Framework is an index that defines how complete the Product Model mapping is. For example, when initially deploying the Flow Framework, the Product Model may only be deployed to one or two value streams, while the remainder of IT work continues with project-oriented management. Visibility and flow metrics are gained for those product lines but not for others. The *alignment index* provides us with a measurement of the portion of work being done by the organization that is connected to a value stream. The higher the index, the more visibility and clearer the mapping to business results.

> **Alignment Index:** The ratio of artifact containers connected to a product value stream relative to all artifact containers across the tool network.

Making Value Streams Visible

With the Value Stream Network in place, all of the flow metrics summarized in Part II can be derived from the flow of artifacts through the network and correlated to business results in order to drive product investment decisions. In addition, the Value Stream Network can be used to optimize value streams themselves, providing the end-to-end visibility that is core to the emerging discipline of value stream management.

As a concrete example of using the Flow Framework for value stream optimization, the following summary reviews five key sources of waste in enterprise value streams, i.e., the "time thieves" summarized by Dominica DeGrandis in her book *Making Work Visible*.[8] DeGrandis describes five time thieves that affect individuals, teams, and organizations. Just as approaches like kanban can make work visible at the team level, the Value Stream Network and associated metrics make work visible at the organizational level and allow teams to react and invest accordingly.

1: Too Much Work in Progress

As Donald Reinertsen points out, limiting WIP is critical to achieving flow in manufacturing.[9] If we put too much WIP on our value streams, queues build up and the rate of delivery decreases. Flow load measures the amount of WIP that we have on each value stream. More importantly, it allows us to see the effects of increased flow load on flow velocity and flow time, and correlates those to see how business results are affected. Experienced product and engineering managers tend to know that higher WIP results in lower velocity, but they struggle to sufficiently push back on the business. The Flow Framework enables a data-driven business case for lowering flow load in order to achieve higher flow velocity by surfacing those metrics for each value stream.

Different value streams may have different tolerances for flow load. For example, a successful product on an insufficiently evolved architecture may have a high degree of unplanned work if developers constantly need to create new architectural components to implement the features being pulled. This can lower that value stream's tolerance for flow load, in contrast with a mature architecture that may be able to tolerate higher flow load. Rather than making generalized assumptions about what WIP limits should be for each value stream, the Value Stream Network provides the data to determine and tune flow load over time.

At Tasktop, we have witnessed this effect by putting too many features that crosscut our architecture on the Hub team. While all of those large and crosscutting features were deemed critical by the business at the time, doing more than one of them in parallel across the teams within that value stream resulted in a lower flow velocity over the course of a year than the flow velocity of taking on one crosscutting feature at a time.

2: Unknown Dependencies

One of the hardest things to manage in software delivery is dependencies between teams, components, and products. DeGrandis identifies three kinds of dependencies: architecture, expertise, and activity based.[10] Each of these dependencies is captured explicitly in the artifact network. For example, if one product team is regularly creating API feature requests from another team, the corresponding artifact relationships will be explicit in the artifact network as an architecture dependency between the two teams. Code reviews and similar review mechanisms in collaboration tools also show up as expertise dependencies in the artifact network. Using this information, it is possible to model dependencies between value streams and look for opportunities to address those dependencies (e.g., by creating a platform value stream that is focused on supporting customer-facing product value streams dependent on a common set of functionality).

In the early days of Tasktop, we used a boutique consulting firm for user experience (UX) design. Features were not flowing quickly enough to meet our time-to-market goals, so we kept hiring more developers to increase flow velocity. However, the gains were lower than we expected. We then examined the Value Stream Network and realized that the bottleneck was not development capacity but the fact that the developers were constantly waiting on wireframes to be produced by the designers. But our developers wouldn't sit idle; they would create user experiences on their own. Given the expectation of the product teams and customers, the demos of the feature set would result in rework to improve the fidelity and ease of the user experience. Due to these flow time issues and the rework that triggered them, we realized that the answer was not to hire more developers but to bring design in house by hiring dedicated UX specialists. We have seen similar bottlenecks with core platform and SDK components that have not had enough staffing to support the number of value streams that depend on them. The more people, teams, and value streams there are, the more difficult it becomes to determine the roots of the dependency problem without a way of visualizing the value streams and their dependencies.

3: Unplanned Work

Unplanned work gets blamed for adding unpredictability to delivery schedules. While the amount of unplanned work can vary across organizations and value streams, the Value Stream Network makes all work visible. Feature and risk work tend to enter at the start of the value stream, as they are planned with business participation. In contrast, an overly high rate of severe incidents or support tickets for a recently launched product can produce defects that land directly on the backlogs of the development team and need to be handled with short flow times. This becomes immediately visible in the flow distribution for that team, making it possible to adjust expectations accordingly while the teams focus on identifying the causes of the unplanned work, such as reducing the technical debt or infrastructure debt that was accrued en route to the initial release.

4: Conflicting Priorities

The Flow Framework surfaces conflicting priorities at the flow item level. For instance, it forces stakeholders to make an explicit decision on how much effort should go to features, defects, risks, and debts. Additionally, it enables the organization to split high-level business priorities into product boundaries that force prioritization based on business objectives and results. However, the work and prioritization within a value stream (e.g., decisions on which features to prioritize for a release) needs to be made in the planning framework that sits a level below the Flow Framework, such as SAFe or Scrum.

5: Neglected Work

DeGrandis points to items such as technical debt and "zombie projects" as wasteful sources of neglected work.[11] Debts are a first-class part of the Flow Framework and form the primary mechanism for allocating time for neglected work. In addition, the activity of defining the Product Model surfaces all of the zombie projects through the alignment index. With those islands of artifacts made visible through the Value Stream Network, the case for end of life or for incorporating them into new or existing value streams becomes explicit and visible.

DeGrandis provides guidance to individuals and teams for finding and eliminating waste in their daily work using tools such as kanban boards and cumulative flow diagrams (CFDs).[12] The Flow Framework and a connected Value Stream Network enable the identification and elimination of the sources of waste across the entire organization.

Conclusion

In this chapter, we defined the final components of the Flow Framework and demonstrated how to create the end-to-end flow that the tech giants and startups of the Age of Software experience by creating a Value Stream Network to leverage best-of-breed tool networks. The Integration Model provides the layer of abstraction over the tool network that allows us to connect the growing number of roles and tools, enabling the automated flow of information across specialists and teams. The Activity Model allows us to map those artifacts and interactions to the flow items and the various stages of the value stream. Finally, the Product Model aligns those flows and activities to the software products in order to measure flow metrics and correlate them to business results. Whereas the lower layers of the network may be highly complex—for example, we have observed many networks with millions of artifacts flowing through the artifact network—the Value Stream Network provides a higher-level, business- and customer-centric view of delivery.

The role of the Value Stream Network is to provide an infrastructure for innovation for software delivery at scale. This completes the managerial framework that we need to transition the organization from project to product, to gain business-level visibility, and to start on the road of optimizing software delivery.

Conclusion to Part III

How was an organization as mature and entrenched as the BMW Group able to bring the electric i3 and i8 to market quickly and successfully?

The level of threat that they perceived from Tesla and other car makers who did not have a gasoline legacy must have been similar to the threat that today's enterprises feel from organizations born in the Age of Software. Even more impressive than the short time to market for the concept vehicles was the BMW Group's ability to scale production to meet market opportunity. For example, in mid-2018, as I wrote this, the BMW Group announced that it was significantly expanding the delivery of Leipzig plant electric models to two hundred per day.[13] As market conditions evolve, the BMW Group is able to adjust its value stream investments accordingly. Why is it that most enterprise IT organizations take so much longer to respond to market changes, even though they are not constrained by the limitations of physical production lines?

In Part III, we uncovered the answer. Without product-oriented value streams, a way of measuring those value streams, and a connected Value Stream Network, the business does not have a direct connection to the technology work that will determine success in the Age of Software. Creating your Value Stream Network is not as difficult as it may sound. When you contrast it to the amount of organizational energy consumed by training every developer on an Agile methodology, it is a fraction of the effort. But it does take a different level of commitment from the business, as this initiative cannot simply be thrown over the wall to IT.

The Flow Framework requires business leaders and technologists to come together and agree on a shared set of metrics that will form the common language and success criteria that the digital business will be managed to. It requires the integration of business planning and management systems with the software delivery tools to create a unified feedback loop. It requires organizations to enable value stream architects who can create and manage this new infrastructure. It requires both empowerment and accountability of the teams working on the value streams to deliver product-oriented business results. And most important, it requires a shift in budgeting and business management away from project to product. Once established, the resulting Value Stream Network will provide the visibility that enables both human and increasingly artificial intelligence to respond to the high pace of change in the market and in the consumer behavior that defines the Turning Point.

The tech giants have already figured this out, and it's time for your organization to as well. Those who commit to managing software delivery as a value-creating software portfolio can survive the Turning Point and thrive in the upcoming Deployment Period. Those who continue in the project-oriented, cost center mentality will increasingly become marginalized as the rest of the economy transitions to the Age of Software.

CONCLUSION

Beyond the Turning Point

'm again sitting on a Boeing 787 Dreamliner, returning to Vancouver from the DevOps Enterprise Summit 2018 in London. Unlike the flight back from the LargeBank meeting two years ago, which had me envisioning billions of dollars of value destroyed as established organizations fumbled their future, I am reflecting on new glimmers of hope.

The enterprise DevOps community was coalesced by Gene Kim and catalyzed by *The Phoenix Project*—the warning flare that signaled to countless IT organizations that it was time for change. While the communities' understanding of the problem is increasing, so is the urgency. During the conference, GE was delisted from the Dow Jones Industrial Average.[1] As of 2017, less than 12% of the Fortune Global 500 companies from 1955 are still on the list.[2] At the current rate of churn, half of the S&P 500 will be replaced over the next ten years.[3] The week of the conference another conversation with Carlota Perez provided further evidence supporting my hypothesis that while we are fifty years into the Age of Software, we have not yet passed through the Turning Point. In Perez's words, "we are still living in the 1930s of the last age."[4]

What will the next twenty years look like for our organizations? Which companies will go extinct in the disruptive chaos of digital change, and which will succeed? How do we direct our organizations to survive and thrive in the Age of Software? The most important reframes of my understanding of how the Age of Software will evolve have come from people with a perspective that spanned ages. Perez was born in 1939 in Venezuela and educated in the US. She witnessed one Deployment Period and its decline and replacement by the next revolution, which shaped her theories on technological revolutions.

In the area of product development, Donald Reinertsen provides a set of concepts learned from mass production that can be applied to the Age of Software and which inspire some of the flow metrics. Finally, Rene Te-Strote showed me firsthand the chasm between the maturity Deployment Period of the Age of Mass Production and the Installation Period of the Age of Software, motivating the focus on business results that is captured in the Flow Framework.

These historical perspectives provide us with the landmarks for the roadmap we need to navigate the next decade. In celebrating its one-hundred-year anniversary in 2016, the BMW Group demonstrated how a company can position itself to thrive in the transition from the Installation Period through the Turning Point by investing in software delivery. Our role is to enable our organizations to do the same.

I have witnessed what happens in the alternative. Xerox was a master of the Age of Mass Production. It amassed enough production capital to fund one of the most innovative research labs of this age, Xerox PARC. While PARC was established in 1970, at the very start of the Installation Period, the visionaries there saw so far into the future of the Age of Software that they created many of the key inventions that catalyzed it. These included the graphical user interface, word processing, modern object-oriented programming, and ethernet networking. However, Xerox failed to capitalize on any of these inventions, dropping them into the hands of companies born in the Age of Software, including Apple and Microsoft.

While on the research staff at PARC, I experienced what it was like to be part of a declining organization. This was made all the more frustrating by the brilliant people who were hanging on due to their clear vision of how the Age of Software would unfold. While PARC's researchers and technologists understood what it took to win in this age, it was the business side of Xerox that was stuck in the managerial models of a previous age and ended up *Fumbling the Future*, as the book on the topic is so aptly named.[5]

I no longer blame those business leaders, as I now realize they were doing their best to navigate the disruption. But they were using the wrong managerial systems to do so. If today's organizations do not learn from this, the story will repeat itself over and over, and organizataional declines similar to those experienced by Xerox will increase.

We have both a corporate and a social responsibility to turn this tide. The tech giants have mastered the new means of production to the point where the consumer and business services they provide are so valuable that attempting to slow progress will be counterproductive. But further increases in the small concentration of both corporate and economic wealth will become even more problematic. While Perez's model predicts that the next crash will result in new regulations that address the imbalance,[6] the majority of the world's large organizations cannot afford to wait that long. We must transform the productivity of our organizations now in order to participate in the manifestation of Perez's ultimate prediction—the post–Turning Point Golden Age, where the benefits of the technological revolution are shared by a broader part of the economy and by society as a whole.

I believe that the Flow Framework is a key part of the solution—a new and effective way to propel a business into the Golden Age. The Flow Framework provides a way to connect tool networks to support end-to-end flow, create an artifact network that provides end-to-end traceability, and create a Value Stream Network that enables the shift from project to product. The flow metrics provide a way of tracking and planning how software investment decisions produce business results and create an organization that can identify bottlenecks and invest accordingly.

This book provides the groundwork to begin the transformation from project-oriented dinosaur to an enterprise that can evolve in a market that is being impacted by immense change on an almost daily basis. The Flow Framework and the shift from project to product will give your organization a new managerial DNA with the plasticity to change and thrive in the Age of Software.

This book is by no means exhaustive. As with any new concept, there are further things to consider in its implementation that will be specific to your organization. For example, the business results of the Flow Framework need to be customized to your business. The Flow Framework does not help with the strategy or design aspects of building great software, as it focuses on enabling the flow and feedback loops needed to enable any kind of digital innovation. In addition, this book stops short of providing technical details needed for Value Stream Architects and other practitioners who are creating and managing Value Stream Networks.

The flow metrics themselves are also only a starting point for making Value Stream Network flows visible. Much richer visualizations are feasible, including real-time and historical playback views that can help identify bottlenecks and areas for optimization. In working with such visualizations, I have realized that the most valuable aspect of a fully connected Value Stream Network is the unified and clean data model of software delivery that it creates. This will be a critical step to progress on analyzing and optimizing software delivery using artificial intelligence techniques with Value Stream Network models as the training set. Finally, modelling the network will enable simulation; for example, to determine the delivery impacts of a company reorganization or acquisition. The Flow Framework provides both the models and the infrastructure guidance to make this possible. Starting the journey now will position you for technological and managerial advances to come.

With any extinction event, the opportunities created in the chaos are enormous. Those who seize the opportunity will be rewarded. By the time detailed playbooks and case studies are written, it will be too late for those who do not shift away from the managerial methods of ages gone by. Will your organization become a fossil, examined after its demise to reveal the lessons of its decline? Or will you make your organization thrive in the Age of Software?

RESOURCES

QUICK REFERENCE FIGURES

Flow Framework™

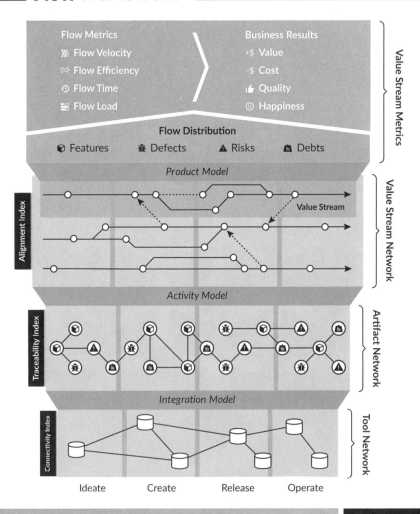

Ideate   Create   Release   Operate

Comparison of Lead Time, Flow Time, and Cycle Time

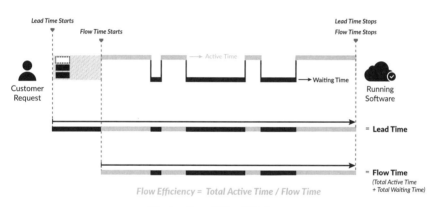

Illustration of Flow Efficiency

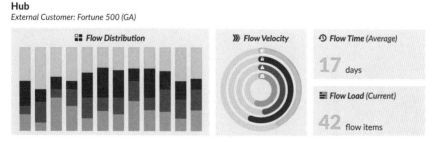

Sample Flow Metrics Dashboard

GLOSSARY

Activity Model: identifies each of the specific activities performed in the value stream and maps those to the concrete workflow states defined by the Integration Model. In addition, it maps these activities to the four flow states, enabling a consistent way of measuring flow across all artifacts.

Age of Mass Production: the technological revolution which occurred between 1908 and 1974 and was marked by advances in the mass production of goods, motorization of transport, oil, gas, synthetic materials, motorways, airports, and airlines.

Age of Software: the current technological revolution, which began in 1971, and is marked by advances in microprocessors, telecommunication, the internet, and software.

Agile: Agile software development is a group of methodologies based on iterative development, where requirements and solutions evolve through the collaboration of self-organizing, cross-functional teams and their customers and end users.

alignment index: the ratio of artifact containers connected to a product value stream relative to all artifact containers across the tool network; this determines the portion of the delivery organization that is aligned to products versus projects.

artifact: a unit of work or delivery defined by one or more tools in the tool network. Artifacts have different types, such as work item, user story, test, or release, which are defined by the artifact schemas in the tools. These types can be instantiated; for example, ten specific user stories can be created for a particular release. Artifacts can be mapped to the more abstract flow units using the integration model.

artifact network: the full network of instantiated artifacts that span the Value Stream Network. The network is connected through artifact relationships, e.g., a requirement may be related to multiple user stories, change sets, and releases.

Business Model disruption: the most profound of Geoffrey Moore's three types of disruption, and one that an established business typically cannot recover from.

connectivity index: the ratio of tool repositories and artifact containers in the tool network that have been integrated to those that have not. The lower the Connectivity Index, the less meaningful the flow metrics are, as the metrics are based on end-to-end flow. For example, flow time cannot be measured without connectivity between the customer request system through to deployment system.

cost center: a department or other unit within an organization to which costs may be charged for accounting purposes; for example, a human resources department. Unlike a profit center, cost centers only contribute to a company's profitability indirectly.

Creative Destruction: the process of industrial mutation, associated with Joseph Schumpeter, that revolutionizes the economy through new innovations and new businesses disrupting and displacing established ones.

Cynefin framework: provides a taxonomy of decision-making contexts, including *obvious*, *complicated*, *complex*, and *chaotic*.

Deployment Period: the period in a technological revolution, following the Installation Period and the Turning Point, where companies that master the means of production earn increasingly larger portions of the economy and the new infrastructure.

digital disruption: the process of established businesses being negatively affected by software-centric companies who displace the entrenched business models with digital offerings. For example, film photography companies like Kodak are being disrupted by digital photography, including via mobile devices.

Extreme Programming: an early flavor of Agile software development that advocates frequent releases in short development cycles.

feature team: a long-lived, cross-functional team that completes end-to-end customer features one by one; core part of the LeSS framework.

First Way of DevOps: flow, as presented in *The DevOps Handbook*.

flow distribution: the proportion of each flow item type within a value stream. The proportion is tracked and adjusted depending on the needs of each product value stream to maximize the business value delivered through that value stream.

flow efficiency: the proportion of time flow items actively worked on to the total time elapsed. This can be used to identify inefficiencies such as overly long wait time for particular flow items.

Flow Framework: a framework for managing software delivery that is focused on measuring and optimizing the flow of business value through product-oriented software value streams that are correlated to business results.

flow item: a unit of business value pulled by a stakeholder through a product's value stream. The four flow items are features, defects, risks and debts.

flow load: number of flow items in a value stream with the flow state of active or waiting. This is analogous to a flow item–based measure of work in progress (WIP) in the value stream. Overly high flow load tends to result in inefficiencies and lead to reduced flow velocity or increased flow time.

flow states: the generic workflow state of a flow item in the value stream. The four flow states are: new, waiting, active, and done. These states are mapped from the concrete workflow states used by a tool, such as "Completed" or "Waiting for Review," using the Activity Model.

flow time: time elapsed from when a flow item enters the value stream (flow state = active) to when it is released to the customer (flow state = done). This corresponds to the total time from when the flow item enters the value stream (i.e., work was started) to when it is completed (i.e., deployed to the customer or end user).

flow velocity: number of flow items completed (i.e., flow state = done) in a given time period.

Incubation Zone: one of Geoffrey Moore's four investment zones where fast growing products and offerings can be incubated prior to producing a material amount of revenue.

Infrastructure Model disruption: involves changes to how customers access a given product or offering. The least disruptive of Geoffrey Moore's three types of disruption and the easiest to adapt an existing business to.

Installation Period: the beginning of a new technological revolution. Marked by large amounts of financial capital, such as venture capital, being deployed to leverage the new technological system that has formed a critical mass of technology, companies, and access to capital that disrupts the organizations that were established in the previous technological revolution.

Integration Model: defines how artifacts flow between one tool and another by mapping the related artifact types to a common artifact model. This enables artifacts, which tend to span multiple tools, to flow through the value stream by having their states synchronized or otherwise integrated.

Kondratiev waves: described as long cycles of economic expansion, stagnation, and recession that result from technological innovation and entrepreneurship.

Lean: a methodology for software development based on Lean manufacturing.

Operating Model disruption: disruptions that rely on changing the relationship of the consumer with the business. One of Geoffrey

Moore's three types of disruption that requires more change from a business to address than the Infrastructure Model Disruption.

Performance Zone: focused on the top line of the business, including the main drivers of revenue; one of Geoffrey Moore's four investment zones.

primary sector: economic sector involving resource extraction from the planet; one of four economic sectors defined by Zoltan Kenessey.

product: a collection of software features and functionality that delivers value to a customer or user. Products can be delivered through multiple mechanisms, e.g., downloadable software, software as a service (SaaS). Products can be external facing, sold to customers; internal facing, such as billing systems; or developer facing, such as a software development toolkit.

Product Model: provides a mapping between the existing artifact containment structure present in the tool network and the product-oriented value streams that are aligned to business value delivery. This enables measuring and tracking all activity, flow metrics, and business results per product.

product value stream: all of the activities spanning all artifacts and tools involved in delivering a specific software product to an internal or external customer.

product-oriented management: management technique that focuses on the continuous delivery of business value through products consumed by internal or external customers.

project-oriented management: management methodology that focuses on the delivery of projects according to a set of milestones, resources, and budget criteria.

production capital: capital that it is controlled by companies producing goods and services; in contrast to capital that is controlled by financial institutions.

Productivity Zone: focused on making the bottom line; one of Geoffrey Moore's four investment zones.

quaternary sector: economic sector involving knowledge work; one of four economic sectors defined by Zoltan Kenessey.

Second Way of DevOps: feedback, as presented in *The DevOps Handbook*.

secondary sector: economic sector involving processing and manufacturing; one of four economic sectors defined by Zoltan Kenessey.

software flow: the activities involved in producing business value along a software value stream.

technical debt: cost of software rework that needs to be incurred at a future time, often coming from a simpler solution being done to complete work instead of applying a better approach that would take longer to complete.

tertiary sector: economic sector involving services; one of four economic sectors defined by Zoltan Kenessey.

Third Way of DevOps: continuous learning, as presented in The DevOps Handbook.

time thieves: the five sources of waste in enterprise value streams as outline by Dominica DeGrandis in *Making Work Visible*.

tool network: the bottom most layer of the Flow Framework, within which the nodes are tools and the links between them are lines of cross-tool integrations.

toolchain: a set of distinct software development tools that are connected, either in a linear chain or a tool network.

traceability index: the measure of artifact connection breadth and depth relative to artifact type. The higher the index, the more connected the artifacts are, enabling improved reporting and visibility.

Transformation Zone: the place in an organization where Incubation Zone products and initiatives can be scaled to a meaningful size for the organization; one of Geoffrey Moore's four investment zones.

value stream: the end-to-end set of activities performed to deliver value to a customer for a product or service. At larger organizations, a value stream tends to span multiple teams, specialists, processes, and tools.

value stream metrics: metrics that measure each value stream within an organization in order for that organization to have a way of correlating software production metrics to business outcomes.

Value Stream Network: the network formed by the connections within and between software value streams. The nodes in this network are the teams of people and other processing units that create business value by working on, processing, and creating artifacts that correspond, either directly or indirectly, to one of the four flow items. Each node corresponds to a particular activity within the value stream, such as development, design, or support. The edges are the connections between the people, processes, and tools along which the flow items progress, from business objective or initiative through to running software. The network can be represented as a directed graph, which can contain cycles. The Value Stream Network is the top of the three network layers and is produced from the tool network and artifact network.

work item: an artifact that encompasses a unit of work to be delivered in the value stream, e.g., a user story or task.

Zone Management: a framework from transforming, modernizing, and reengineering a business created by Geoffrey Moore.

NOTES

Introduction: The Turning Point

1. Carlota Perez, *Technological Revolutions and Financial Capital: The Dynamics of Bubbles and Golden Ages* (Cheltenham, UK: Edward Elgar, 2003), 5.
2. Perez, *Technological Revolutions and Financial Capital*, 114.
3. Adapted from Perez, *Technological Revolutions and Financial Capital*, 78.
4. Scott D. Anthony, S. Patrick Vinguerie, Evan I. Schwartz, and John Van Landeghem, "2018 Corporate Longevity Forecast: Creative Destruction is Accelerating," Innosight website, accessed on June 22, 2018, https://www.innosight.com/insight/creative-destruction/.
5. Mik Kersten, "Mining the Ground Truth of Enterprise Toolchains," *IEEE Software* 35, no. 3 (2018): 12–17.
6. Gene Kim, Patrick Debois, John Willis, and Jez Humble, *The DevOps Handbook: How to Create World-Class Agility, Reliability, and Security in Technology Organizations* (Portland, OR: IT Revolution, 2016), 114.
7. "Digital Taylorism: A Modern Version of 'Scientific Management' Threatens to Dehumanise the Workplace," *The Economist*, September 10, 2015, https://www.economist.com/business/2015/09/10/digital-taylorism.

Part I: Introduction

1. Robert N. Charette, "This Car Runs on Code," *IEEE Spectrum*, February 1, 2009, https://spectrum.ieee.org/transportation/systems/this-car-runs-on-code.
2. Michael Sheetz, "Technology Killing Off Corporate America: Average Life Span of Companies Under 20 Years," *CNBC*, August 24, 2018, https://www.cnbc.com/2017/08/24/technology-killing-off -corporations-average-lifespan-of -company-under-20-years.html.

Chapter 1

1. Matthew Garrahan, "Google and Facebook Dominance Forecast to Rise," *Financial Times*, December 3, 2017, https://www.ft.com/content/cf362186 -d840-11e7-a039-c64b1c09b482.

2. Lauren Thomas, "Amazon Grabbed 4 Percent of all US Retail Sales in 2017, New Study Says," *CNBC*, January 3, 2018, https://www.cnbc.com/2018/01/03 /amazon-grabbed-4-percent-of-all-us-retail-sales-in-2017-new-study.html.

3. Lily Hay Newman, "6 Fresh Horrors from the Equifax CEO's Congressional Hearing," *Wired*, October 3, 2017, https://www.wired.com/story /equifax-ceo-congress-testimony.

4. Andreas Bubenzer-Paim, "Why No Industry is Safe From Tech Disruption," *Forbes*, November 7, 2017, https://www.forbes.com/sites/forbestechcouncil/2017 /11/07/why-no-industry-is-safe-from-tech-disruption/#5f8a995530d3.

5. Brian Solis and Aubrey Littleton, "The 2017 State of Digital Transformation," Altimeter, October 2017, https://marketing.prophet.com/acton/media/33865 /altimeter—the-2017-state-of-digital-transformation.

6. Gene Kim, personal communication with Mik Kersten, 2017.

7. Alan Kay, as quoted in Erika Andersen, "Great Leaders Don't Predict the Future—They Invent It," *Forbes*, July 10, 2013, https://www.forbes .com/sites/erikaandersen/2013/07/10/great-leaders-dont-predict-the-future -they-invent-it/#275484926840.

8. Jeff Dunn, "Tesla is Valued as High as Ford and GM—But That has Nothing to do with What It's Done so Far," *Business Insider*, April 11, 2017, http://www .businessinsider.com/tesla-value-vs-ford-gm -chart-2017-4.

9. "The Future has Begun," BMW website, accessed June 22, 2018, https://www .bmwgroup.com/en/next100.html.

10. Edward Taylor and Ilona Wissenbach, "Exclusive—At 100, BMW Sees Radical New Future in World of Driverless Cars," *Reuters*, March 3, 2016, https://www .reuters.com/article/autoshow-geneva-software/exclusive-at-100-bmw-sees -radical-new-future-in-world-of-driverless-cars-idUSKCN0W60HP.

11. Zoltan Kenessey, "The Primary, Secondary, Tertiary and Quaternary Sectors of the Economy," *The Review of Income and Wealth: Journal of the International Association*, 1987, http://www.roiw.org/1987/359.pdf.

12. Cade Metz, "Google is 2 Billion Lines of Code—And it's All in One Place," *Wired*, September 16, 2015, https://www.wired.com/2015/09/google-2-billion -lines-codeand-one-place.

13. Charette, "This Car Runs on Code."

14. "Bosch Plans More than 20,000 Hires," Bosch press release, March 24, 2015, https://www.bosch-presse.de/pressportal/de/en/bosch-plans-more-than-20000 -hires-98560.html.

15. Ashley Rodriguez, "Netflix Was Born Out of This Grad-School Math Problem," *Quartz*, February 28, 2017, https://qz.com/921205/netflix-ceo-reed-hastings-predicted-the-future-of-video-from-considering-this-grad-school-math-problem/.

16. Marc Andreessen, "Why Software is Eating the World," *Wall Street Journal*, August 20, 2011, https://www.wsj.com/articles/SB10001424053111903480904576512250915629460.

17. therealheisenberg, "'Greedy Bastards': Amazon, Whole Foods Deal 'Changes Everything,'" *Heisenberg Report*, June 16, 2017, https://heisenbergreport.com/2017/06/16/greedy-bastards-amazon-whole-foods-deal-changes-everything/.

18. Geoffrey Moore, *Zone to Win: Organizing to Compete in an Age of Disruption*, iBook edition (New York: Diversion Publishing, 2015), Chapter 2.

19. Moore, *Zone to Win*, Chapter 1.

20. "Catherine Bessant," Bank of America website, https://newsroom.bankofamerica.com/cathy-bessant.

21. Jean Baptise Su, "The Global Fintech Landscape Reaches Over 1000 Companies," *Forbes*, September 28, 2016, https://www.forbes.com/sites/jeanbaptiste/2016/09/28/the-global-fintech-landscape-reaches-over-1000-companies-105b-in-funding-867b-in-value-report/#de39e1f26f3d.

22. Joseph Schumpeter, *Capitalism, Socialism and Democracy*, Third Edition (New York: Harper Perennial Modern Classics, 2008), 81.

23. Perez, *Technological Revolutions and Financial Capital*, 37.

24. "Catch the Wave: The Long Cycles of Industrial Innovation are Becoming Shorter," *The Economist*, February 18, 1999, https://www.economist.com/node/186628.

25. Jerry Neumann, "The Deployment Age," *The Reaction Wheel: Jerry Neumann's Blog*, October 14 2015, http://reactionwheel.net/2015/10/the-deployment-age.html.

26. Perez, *Technological Revolutions and Financial Capital*, 11; Chris Freeman and Francisco Louçã, *As Time Goes By: From the Industrial Revolution to the Information Revolution* (Oxford: Oxford University Press, 2001).

27. Perez, *Technological Revolutions and Financial Capital*, 11.

28. Perez, *Technological Revolutions and Financial Capital*, 37.

29. Carlota Perez, personal communication/unpublished interview with Mik Kersten, April 18, 2018.

30. Adapted from Perez, *Technological Revolutions and Financial Capital*, 11; Freeman and Louçã, *As Time Goes By*.

31. "Jawbone is the Second Costliest VC-Backed Startup Death Ever," *CBInsights*, July 12, 2017, https://www.cbinsights.com/research/jawbone-second-costliest-startup-fail.

32. Steven Levy, "The Inside Story Behind Pebble's Demise," *Wired*, December 12, 2016, https://www.wired.com/2016/12/the-inside-story-behind-pebbles-demise.

33. Steve Toth, "66 Facebook Acquisitions—The Complete List (2018)," *TechWyse*, January 4, 2018, https://www.techwyse.com/blog/infographics/facebook-acquisitions-the-complete-list-infographic.

34. Mik Kersten and Gail C. Murphy, "Using Task Context to Improve Programmer Productivity," *Proceedings of the 14th ACM SIGSOFT International Symposium on Foundations of Software Engineering* (November 5–11, 2006): 1–11, https://www.tasktop.com/sites/default/files/2006-11-task-context-fse.pdf.

35. Kersten and Murphy, "Using Task Context to Improve Programmer Productivity," 1–11.

36. Brian Palmer, "How Did Detroit Become Motor City," *Slate*, February 29, 2012, http://www.slate.com/articles/news_and_politics/explainer/2012/02/why_are_all_the_big_american_car_companies_based_in_michigan_.html.

Chapter 2

1. Bob Parker, "Modeling the Future Enterprise: People, Purpose and Profit," *Infor*, January 10, 2018, http://blogs.infor.com/insights/2018/01/modeling-the-future-enterprise-people-purpose-and-profit.html.

2. Bernard Marr, "What Everyone Must Know About Industry 4.0," *Forbes*, June 20, 2016, https://www.forbes.com/sites/bernardmarr/2016/06/20/what-everyone-must-know-about-industry-4-0/#37319d2a795f.

3. Horatiu Boeriu, "BMW Celebrates 1.5 Billion Cars Built at Leipzig Plant," *BMW BLOG*, October 26, 2014, http://www.bmwblog.com/2014/10/26/bmw-celebrates-1-5-million-cars-built-leipzig-plant/.

4. "The Nokia Test," *LeanAgileTraining.com*, December 2, 2007, https://www.leanagiletraining.com/better-agile/the-nokia-test.

5. James Surowiecki, "Where Nokia Went Wrong," *The New Yorker*, September 3, 2013, https://www.newyorker.com/business/currency/where-nokia-went-wrong.

6. Kent Beck with Cynthia Andres, *Extreme Programming Explained: Embrace Change*, Second Edition (Boston, MA: Addison-Wesley, November 16, 2004), 85.

7. Eliyahu M. Goldratt and Jeff Cox, *The Goal: A Process of Ongoing Improvement*, (New York: Routledge, 1984) Kindle location 2626 and 6575.

8. Kim, Debois, Willis, and Humble, *The DevOps Handbook*, 1.

9. Mik Kersten, "How to Guarantee Failure in Your Agile DevOps Transformation," Tasktop blog, June 24, 2016, https://www.tasktop.com/blog/how-to-guarantee-failure-in-your-agile-devops-transformation/.

10. Jason Del Rey, "This is the Jeff Bezos Playbook for Preventing Amazon's Demise," *Recode*, April 12, 2017, https://www.recode.net/2017/4/12/15274220/jeff-bezos-amazon-shareholders-letter-day-2-disagree-and-commit.

11. "World Class Supplier Quality," Boeing website, accessed July 27, 2018, http://787updates.newairplane.com/787-Suppliers/World-Class-Supplier-Quality.

12. "World Class Supplier Quality," Boeing website, accessed July 27, 2018, http://787updates.newairplane.com/787-Suppliers/World-Class-Supplier-Quality.

13. Gail Murphy, personal communication with Mik Kersten, 1997.

14. Mike Sinnett, "787 No-Bleed Wystems: Saving Fuel and Enhancing Operational Efficiencies," *AERO Magazine*, 2007, https://www.boeing.com/commercial/aeromagazine/articles/qtr_4_07/AERO_Q407.pdf.

15. Bill Rigby and Tim Hepher, "Brake Software Latest Threat to Boeing 787," *Reuters*, July 15, 2008, https://www.reuters.com/article/us-airshow-boeing-787/brake-software-latest-threat -to-boeing-787-idUSL155973002000.

16. Anonymous, personal communication with Mik Kersten, 2008.

17. Rigby and Hepher, "Brake Software Latest Threat."

18. Rigby and Hepher, "Brake Software Latest Threat."

19. Rigby and Hepher, "Brake Software Latest Threat."

20. Rigby and Hepher, "Brake Software Latest Threat."

21. Mary Poppendieck, "The Cost Center Trap," *The Lean Mindset* blog, November 5, 2017, http://www.leanessays.com/2017/11/the-cost-center-trap.html.

22. Jason Paur, "Boeing 747 Gets an Efficiency Makeover to Challenged A380," *Wired*, January 10, 2010, https://www.wired.com/2010/01/boeing-747-gets-an -efficient-makeover-to-challenge-a380.

23. Donald Reinertsen, *The Principles of Product Development Flow: Second Generation Lean Product Development* (Redondo Beach, CA: Celeritas, 2009), Kindle location 177.

24. Moore, *Zone to Win*, Chapter 2.

25. Moore, *Zone to Win*, Chapter 2.

26. Scott Span, "Happy People = Higher Profits: Lessons from Henry Ford in Business and Leadership," *Tolero Solutions*, accessed on May 24, 2018, http://www.tolerosolutions.com/happy-people-higher-profits-lessons-from-henry-ford-in -business-leadershi.

27. John Willis, "The Andon Cord," IT Revolution blog, October 15, 2015, https://itrevolution.com/kata/.

28. David J. Snowden and Mary E. Boone, "A Leader's Framework for Decision Making," *Harvard Business Review*, November 2007, https://hbr.org/2007/11/a-leaders-framework-for-decision-making.

29. Bruce W. Tuckman, "Developmental Sequence in Small Groups," *Psychological Bulletin* 63, no. 6 (1965): 384–399.

30. Marc Löffler, "Watermelon Reporting," *DZone*, August 8, 2011, https://dzone.com/articles/watermelon-reporting.

Chapter 3

1. Scott Galloway, *The Four: The Hidden DNA of Amazon, Apple, Facebook, and Google* (New York, NY: Random House, 2017), 28.

2. James Womack and Daniel Jones, *Lean Thinking: Banish Waste and Create Wealth in Your Corporation*, Third Edition (New York: Free Press, 2003), 10.

3. Womack and Jones, *Lean Thinking*, 10.

4. Mike Rother and John Shook, *Learning to See: Value Stream Mapping to Add Value and Eliminate MUDA* (Cambridge, MA: Lean Enterprise Institute, 2003), 3.

5. Kersten, "Mining the Ground Truth of Enterprise Toolchains."

6. John Allspaw, "How Your Systems Keep Running Day after Day," Keynote Address at DevOps Enterprise Summit 2017, San Francisco, November 15, 2017.

7. Philippe Kruchten, Robert Nord, and Ipek Ozkaya, "Technical Debt: From Metaphor to Theory and Practice," *IEEE Software* 29, no. 6 (2012), 18–21.

8. Kaimar Karu, *ITIL and DevOps—Getting Started* (Axelos, 2007).

9. Dean Leffingwell, *SAFe 4.0 Distilled: Applying the Scaled Agile Framework for Lean Software and Systems Engineering* (Boston, MA: Addison-Wesley, 2017), 243.

PART II

Chapter 4

1. Perez, *Technological Revolutions and Financial Capital*, ix.

2. Steve Coley, "Enduring Ideas: The Three Horizons of Growth," *McKinsey Quarterly*, December 2009, https://www.mckinsey.com/business-functions -functions/strategy-and-corporate-finance/our-insights/enduring-ideas-the -three-horizons-of-growth.

3. Fred P. Brooks, Jr., *The Mythical Man-Month: Essays on Software Engineering* (Boston, MA: Addison-Wesley, 1995).

4. Margaret Rouse, "Agile Velocity," *TechTarget*, July 2013, https://whatis.tech target.com/definition/Agile-velocity.

5. Leffingwell, *SAFe 4.0 Distilled*, 95.

6. Nicole Forsgren, PhD, Jez Humble, Gene Kim, *Accelerate: The Science of Lean Software and DevOps: Building and Scaling High Performing Technology Organizations* (Portland, OR: IT Revolution Press, 2018), 11

7. Tara Hamilton-Whitaker, "Agile Estimation and the Cone of Uncertainty," *Agile 101*, August 18, 2009, https://agile101.wordpress.com/tag/t-shirt-sizing/.

8. Margaret Rouse, "Law of Large Numbers," TechTarget, Decem- ber 2012, https:// whatis.techtarget.com/definition/law-of-large-numbers.

9. Frederic Paul, "Gene Kim Explains 'Why DevOps Matters,'" *New Relic*, June 24, 2015, https://blog.newrelic.com/2015/06/24/gene-kim-why-devops-matters/.

10. Dominica DeGrandis, *Making Work Visible: Exposing Time Theft to Optimize Work and Flow* (Portland, OR: IT Revolution, 2017), 142.

11. Carmen DeArdo, "On the Evolution of Agile to DevOps," *CIO Review*, accessed on June 26, 2018, https://devops.cioreview.com/cxoinsight/on-the-evolution-of -agile-to-devops-nid-26383-cid-99.html.

12. DeGrandis, *Making Work Visible*, 8–15.
13. Reinertsen, *The Principles of Product Development Flow*, Kindle location 1192.
14. Reinertsen, *The Principles of Product Development Flow*, Kindle location 147.
15. Eliyahu M. Goldratt, "Standing on the Shoulders of Giants," as featured in *The Goal: A Process of Ongoing Improvement*, Kindle edition (Great Barrington, MA: North River Press, 1992), Kindle location 6293.
16. Reinertsen, *The Principles of Product Development Flow*, Kindle location 1030.
17. DeGrandis, *Making Work Visible*, 141–154.

Chapter 5

1. Camilla Knudsen and Alister Doyle, "Norway Powers Ahead (Electrically): Over Half New Car Sales Now Electric or Hybrid," *Reuters*, January 3, 2018, https://www.reuters.com/article/us-environment-norway-autos/norway-powers-ahead-over-half-new-car-sales-now-electric-or-hybrid-idUSKBN1ES0WC.
2. "BMW Expands Leipzig Factory to 200 BMW i Models Daily", *Eletrive*, May 24, 2018, https://www.electrive.com/2018/05/24/bmw-expands-leipzig-factory-to-200-bmw-i-models-daily.
3. Bruce Baggaley, "Costing by Value Stream," *Journal of Cost Management* 18, no. 3 (May/June 2013), 24–30.
4. Reinertsen, *The Principles of Product Development Flow*, Kindle location 177.
5. Nicole Forsgren, Jez Humble, Gene Kim, Alanna Brown, and Nigel Kersten, *2017 State of DevOps Report* (Puppet, 2018), https://puppet.com/resources/whitepaper/state-of-devops-report.
6. Daniel Pink, Drive: *The Surprising Truth About What Motivates Us* (New York: Riverhead Books, 2011), 1–10.
7. Forsgren, Humble, Kim, *Accelerate*, 102.
8. Fred Reichheld, *The Ultimate Question 2.0 (Revised and Expanded Edition): How Net Promoter Companies Thrive in a Customer-Driven World* (Boston, MA: Harvard Business School Press, 2011), Kindle location 2182.

Chapter 6

1. Charette, "This Car Runs on Code."
2. Charette, "This Car Runs on Code."
3. Neil Steinkamp, *Industry Insights for the Road Ahead: 2016 Automotive Warranty & Recall Report*, (Stout Rissus Ross, Inc, 2016), https://www.stoutadvisory.com/insights/report/2016-automotive-warranty-recall-report.
4. Steinkamp, *Industry Insights for the Road Ahead*.
5. History.com Staff "Automobile History," History Channel website, 2010, https://www.history.com/topics/automobiles.

6. John Hunter, "Deming's 14 Points for Management," *The W. Edwards Deming Institute Blog*, April 15, 2013, https://blog.deming.org/2013/04/demings-14-points-for-management.

7. "Computer Aided Engineering at BMW, Powered by High Performance Computing 2nd," Slideshare.net, posted by Fujitsu Global, November 19, 2015, slide 29, https://www.slideshare.net/FujitsuTS/computer-aided-engineering-at-bmw-powered-by-high-performance-computing-2nd.

8. Viktor Reklaitis, "How the Number of Data Breaches is Soaring—In One Chart," *MarketWatch*, May 25, 2018, https://www.marketwatch.com/story/how-the-number-of-data-breaches-is-soaring-in-one-chart-2018-02-26.

9. Joan Weiner, "Despite Cyberattacks at JPMorgan, Home Depot and Target, Many Millenials Aren't Worried About Being Hacked," *The Washington Post*, October 8, 2014, https://www.washingtonpost.com/blogs/she-the-people/wp/2014/10/08/despite-cyberattacks-at-jpmorgan-home-depot-and-target-many-millennials-arent-worried-about-being-hacked/?noredirect=on&utm_terms=.97579f2f101c.

10. Erica R. Hendry, "How the Equifax Hack Happened, According to its CEO," *PBS News Hour*, October 3, 2017, https://www.pbs.org/newshour/nation/equifax-hack-happened-according-ceo.

11. Lily Hay Newman, "6 Fresh Horrors from the Equifax CEO's Congressional Hearing," *Wall Street Journal*, October 3, 2017, https://www.wired.com/story/equifax-ceo-congress-testimony.

12. Lorenzo Franceshi-Bicchierai, "Equifax was Warned," *Motherboard*, October 26, 2018, https://motherboard.vice.com/en_us/article/ne3bv7/equifax-breach-social-security-numbers-researcher-warning.

13. Tom Kranzit, "Nokia Completes Symbian," *CNET*, December 2, 2008, https://www.cnet.com/news/nokia-completes-symbian-acquisition.

14. Ward Cunningham, "The WyCash Portfolio Management System," *OOPSLA 1992*, March 26, 1992, http://c2.com/doc/oopsla92.html.

15. Steve O'Hear, "Nokia buys Symbian, Opens Fire on Android, Windows Mobile and iPhone," *Last100*, June 24, 2008, http://www.last100.com/2008/06/24/nokia-buys-symbian-opens-fire-on-google-android-and-iphone/.

16. Shira Ovide, "Deal is Easy Part for Microsoft and Nokia," *Wall Street Journal*, September 3, 2018, https://www.wsj.com/articlesmicrosoft-buys-nokia-mobile-business-in-7-billion-deal-1378188311.

17. "Microsoft to Acquire Nokia's Devices and Services Business, License Nokia's Patents and Mapping Services," Microsoft website, September 3, 2013, https://news.microsoft.com/2013/09/03/microsoft-to-acquire-nokias-devices-services-business-license-nokias-patents-and-mapping-services/.

18. Chris Ziegler, "Nokia CEO Stephan Elop Rallies Troops in Brutally Honest 'Burning Platform' Memo (Update: It's Real!)," *Engadget*, August 2, 2011,

https://www.engadget.com/2011/02/08/nokia-ceo-stephe-elop-rallies-troops
-in-brutally-honest-burnin.

19. Philip Michaels, "Jobs: OS 9 is Dead, Long Live OS X," *Macworld*, May 1, 2002, https://www.macworld.com/article/1001445/06wwdc.html.

20. "The Internet Tidal Wave," *Letters of Note*, July 22, 2011, http://www.letters ofnote.com/2011/07/internet-tidal-wave.html.

21. Bill Gates, "Memo from Bill Gates," *Microsoft*, January 11, 2012, https://news .microsoft.com/2012/01/11/memo-from-bill-gates.

22. "Microsoft Promises End to 'DLL Hell,'" *CNet*, March 7, 2003, https://www.cnet .com/news/microsoft-promises-end-to-dll-hell/.

23. David Bank, "Borland Charges Microsoft Stole Away Its Employees," *The Wall Street Journal*, May 8, 1997, https://www.wsj.com/articles/SB863034062733665000.

24. Rene Te-Strote, personal communication/unpublished interview with Mik Kersten, April 20, 2017.

25. Stephen O'Grady, *The New Kingmakers: How Developers Conquered the World* (Sebastopol, CA: O'Reilly Media, 2013), 5.

PART III

1. "Agile at Microsoft," YouTube video, 41:04, posted by Microsoft Visual Studio, October 2, 2017, https://www.youtube.com/watch?v =-LvCJpnNljU.

3. Forsgren, Humble, and Kim, *Accelerate*, 66.

Chapter 7

1. History.com staff, "Automobile History."

2. Alex Davies, "Telsa Ramps up Model 3 Production and Predicts Profits this Fall," *Wired*, May 2, 2018, https://www.wired.com/story/tesla-model-3 -production-profitability.

3. Womack and Jones, *Lean Thinking*, Chapter 11.

4. Mik Kersten and Gail C. Murphy, "Mylar: A Degree-of-Interest Model for IDEs," *Proceedings of the 4th International Conference on Aspect-Oriented Software Development* (March 14–18, 2005): 159–168.

5. Mik Kersten, "Lessons Learned from 10 Years of Application Lifecyle Management," *InfoQ*, December 24, 2015, https://www.infoq.com/articles /lessons-application-lifecycle.

Chapter 8

1. Mik Kersten, "Mik Kersten Keynote on the Future of ALM: Developing in the Social Code Graph (EclipseCon 2012)," YouTube video, 47:55, posted by Tasktop, April 10, 2012, https://www.youtube.com/watch?v=WBwyAyvneNo.

2. Nicole Forsgren, PhD, and Mik Kersten, PhD, "DevOps Metrics: Your Biggest Mistake Might be Collecting the Wrong Data," *ACM Queue* 15, no. 6 (2017), https://queue.acm.org/detail.cfm?id=3182626.

3. Kersten, "Mining the Ground Truth of Enterprise Toolchains," 12–17.

4. Perez, *Technological Revolutions and Financial Capital*, 114.

5. Danny Palmer, "What is GDPR? Everything You Need to Know About the New General Data Protection Regulations," *ZDNet*, May 23, 2018, https://www.zdnet.com/article/gdpr-an-executive-guide-to-what-you-need-to-know.

6. Rachel Potvin and Josh Levenber, "Why Google Stores Billions of Lines of Code in a Single Repository," *Communications of the ACM* 59, no. 7 (2016): 78–87, https://cacm.acm.org/magazines/2016/7/204032-why-google-stores-billions-of-lines-of-code-in-a-single-repository/fulltext.

7. Internal Tasktop Report, unpublished, 2018.

8. "Life Expectancy," *Wikipedia*, last modified June 20, 2018, https://en.wikipedia.org/wiki/Life_expectancy.

9. "Careers in Medicine," Association of American Medical Colleges website, accessed August 23, 2018, http://www.aamc.org/cim/speciality/exploreoptions/list/.

10. General Stanley McChrystal, *Team of Teams: New Rules of Engagement for a Complex World* (New York: Portfolio, 2015), iBook Chapter 6.

11. "Study Suggests Medical Errors Now Third Leading Cause of Death in the U.S.," *Johns Hopkins Medicine*, May 3, 2016, https://www.hopkinsmedicine.org/news/media/releases/study_suggests_medical_errors_now_third_leading_cause_of_death_in_the_us.

12. "Supplier Management," BMW Group website, accessed July 1, 2018, https://www.bmwgroup.com/en/responsibility/supply-chain-management.html.

Chapter 9

1. Reinertsen, *The Principles of Product Development Flow*, Kindle location 391.

2. Gary Gruver and Tommy Mouser, *Leading the Transformation: Applying Agile and DevOps Principles at Scale* (Portland, OR: IT Revolution, 2015), 20–25.

3. Goldratt and Cox, *The Goal*, Kindle location 2626 and 6575.

4. "Metcalfe's Law," *Wikipedia*, last updated June 15, 2018, https://en.wikipedia.org/wiki/Metcalfe%27s_law.

5. Christopher Condo and Diego LoGiudice, *Elevate Agile-Plus-DevOps with Value Stream Management*, Forrester Research, Inc., May 11, 2018.

6. Anonymous, personal communication with Mik Kersten, 2017.

7. Carliss Baldwin, Kim B. Clark, Carliss Y. Baldwin, *The Option Value of Modularity in Design* (Boston, MA: Harvard Business School, 2002).

8. DeGrandis, *Making Work Visible*, 1.

9. Reinertsen, *The Principles of Product Development Flow*, Kindle location 132.

10. DeGrandis, *Making Work Visible*, 17.
11. DeGrandis, *Making Work Visible*, 25.
12. DeGrandis, *Making Work Visible*, 39.
13. Fred Lambery, "BMW to Increase "BMW i' Electric Vehicle Production by 54%," *electrek*, May 25, 2018, http://electrek.co/2018/05/25/bmw-i-electric-vehicle -production/.

Conclusion

1. Sarah Ponczek and Rick Clough, "GE Kicked Out of Dow, the Last 19th Century Member Removed," *Bloomberg*, June 19, 2018, updated on June 20, 2018, https://www.bloomberg.com/news/articles/2018-06-19/ge-gets-kicked-out-of -dow-the-last-19th-century-member-removed.
2. Mark J. Perry, "Fortune 500 Firms 1955 v. 2017: Only 60 Remain, Thanks to the Creative Destruction That Fuels Economic Prosperity," *AEIdeas*, October 20, 2017, http://www.aei.org/publication/fortune-500-firms-1955-v-2017-only-12 -remain-thanks-to-the-creative-destruction-that-fuels-economic-prosperity/.
3. Scott D. Anthony, S. Patrick Viguerie, Evan I Schwartz, and John Van Dandeghem, *2018 Corporate Longevity Forecast: Creative Destruction is Accelerating*, accessed August 15, 2018, https://www.innosight.com/insight/creative-destruction/
4. Carlota Perez, personal communication with Mik Kersten, June 27, 2018.
5. Douglas K. Smith and Robert C. Alexander, *Fumbling the Future: How Xerox Invented, Then Ignored, the First Personal Computer* (Bloomington, IN: iUniverse, Inc., 1999).
6. Perez, *Technological Revolutions and Financial Capital*, 114.

INDEX

ACKNOWLEDGMENTS

This book builds on the literary work of those who have shaped my understanding of technology and management, including Steve Blank, Fred Brooks, Clayton Christenson, Peter Drucker, Geoffrey Moore, Carlota Perez, and Donald Reinertsen. The following is a list of people who helped me build on those ideas and contributed directly to the ideation, creation, and release of this book.

First, there are two people who catalyzed this book into existence. Neelan Choksi saw the opportunity for the industry to think in a new way about software and kept pushing me to write a book on that. I kept pushing back, but he did not give up. Along with Simon Bodymore, Neelan provided the support I needed to write while running a company (if I had properly predicted how writing this book would be, however, I probably would have pushed back harder).

The second person who made for this book possible is Gene Kim. I will never forget approaching Gene at a conference in the fall of 2016 and telling him that I wanted to write a book on integration patterns. Not only did he hear me out but he realized these ideas were tied to a much bigger tectonic shift. He became an advisor and intellectual sparring partner to me in the months following. Gene challenged me to write a much more ambitious book than I was envisioning and to go beyond the technologists and reach the business side. In our regular brainstorming sessions (which felt more like brain hurricaning), many of the key ideas in this book were hashed out. In addition to introducing me to the work of Carlota Perez, Gene introduced me to many of the thought leaders that make up the DevOps community. The term *scenius* (coined by musician Brian Eno) describes great works that are created from a community of motivated and mutually appreciative individuals; I would like to thank Gene for creating the scenius that made this book possible. And *Project to Product* builds on other products of that scenius, including Dominica DeGrandis' *Making Work Visible*, Nicole Forsgren et al.'s *Accelerate*, Gene Kim et al.'s *The DevOps Handbook* and *The Phoenix Project*, and Mark Schwartz's *The Art of Business Value* and *A Seat at the Table*.

The work and results of this book came from a decade of product development at Tasktop, to which I have my many colleagues to thank. Nicole Bryan and Robert Elves have been shaping and reshaping the vision of the Flow Framework, constantly iterating through customer discussions, product development, and experimentation. In the early days of Tasktop, it was Nicole who took me through the transition of project thinking to product thinking, and she continued to guide me and our delivery practices and products. Robert Elves has been pursuing flow and productivity with me—both in terms of ideas and code—since we were pursuing graduate degrees. In the early days, it was just me and Rob coding the open-source Eclipse Mylyn project, and it has been amazing to witness how far his ideas have come. The Flow Framework is the tip of the conceptual iceberg that Nicole and Rob have been creating and proving with enterprise customers for the better part of a decade.

I would also like to thank the other Tasktop staff whose ideas and feedback have been instrumental to this book, including Dominica DeGrandis, Naomi Lurie, Adrian Jones, and Wesley Coelho. Patrick Anderson helped tremendously on the research and citations. Zhen Wang created the figures and helped uncover ways to simplify the concepts as we turned them into visual form.

The book speaks of epiphanies, those wonderful moments when the ideas flowing around in our minds suddenly anneal into a consistent and compelling form. For me, those times have come from countless conversations with mentors and the other influencers who have changed my perspective. By far, the person who has been most perspective changing is Gail Murphy—her contributions to this work are innumerable. When she taught me software engineering in my undergraduate years, Gail inspired in me the need to frame our work around how technology solves world problems before diving deep into the technical ones. Gail founded Tasktop with me and Rob, and she has constantly challenged me and helped me think. Most important, she created the scenius at the University of British Columbia Software Practices Lab that enabled both me and many other PhD students to do a new kind of research focused on learning from the ground truth of empirical data in software tool networks.

Gail introduced me to Gregor Kiczales, who recruited me to Xerox PARC and the two of them reshaped my views on building software. At a conceptual level, the Flow Framework is an application of Gregor's ideas around crosscutting modularity to software value streams. Gregor then introduced me to Carliss Baldwin, whose work at Harvard Business School allowed me to frame these ideas in an economic context. The book is also heavily influenced by Rod Johnson's ideas about software modularity, as well Charles Simonyi's; each of them pursued a bigger and better view of modularity than what existed, and I learned a tremendous amount working with them on their journeys.

I am also grateful for the work and feedback of Carlota Perez, who has provided a model of technological progress that I hope more future technologists frame their work in.

A majority of my inspiration for this book came from the many conversations I've had with IT leaders and practitioners looking for a better way. No conversations stand out more than those that I had with Carmen DeArdo of Nationwide Insurance. While at Bell Labs, Carmen gained a view of what software delivery should look like. He has taught me more of that vision, along with his views on the concepts of value streams and flow, every time I've met with him. The entire challenge for creating a framework that would stop organization's pursuing local optimizations of the value stream was inspired by Carmen.

Similar to Carmen's teachings on enterprise-scale IT, Dave West has been my mentor for all things Agile. Dave's ideas about finding a better way to do Agile product development have helped shaped my understanding, and they continue to do so through our discussions. Dave provided invaluable feedback on the early drafts of this book and helped challenge and refine the key ideas.

More recently, the ideas and practices that Jon Smart has been putting in place have been pushing my understanding of how Lean practices work at scale. Jon's feedback and his approach of avoiding big bang transformations at Barclays in favor of "better value faster, safer, and happier" have been an input to some aspects of the Flow Framework.

Ross Clanton and Bjorn-Freeman Benson provided helpful guidance on both sides of the project-and-product equation. In addition, Sam Guckenheimer is one of the best critical thinkers in this space, continually pushing me on key ideas, and his input has helped evolve the entire framing of the journey for going from project to product.

Rene Te-Strote gets a special thank you for opening my eyes to what the culmination of the last age of production looked like. Without all of the years of discussions with him, I do not think I would have had an appreciation for the magnitude of the gap.

I am also very grateful to the passion for production and professionalism of Frank Schäfer, who took us on the BMW Leipzig plant trip and answered the hundreds of questions that lasted two days.

In terms of connecting the ideas of flow to the business, Ralf Waltram has been a great sparring partner, sharing the mission of getting software delivery to the level of excellence that we know from advanced manufacturing. The title of the book came from Ralf during a discussion in which we were trying to better understand this fundamental mismatch.

The book would not be what it is without Anna Noak's amazing ideas, editing, and coaching. Anna mentored me, pushed me, and was instrumental in making this book what it is, from the first idea to the final edits we completed face-to-face in Portland. Big thanks also go to the other IT Revolution staff who worked on the book. A special thank you to Devon Smith for his great cover and interior design, and to the editors: Kate Sage, Karen Brattain, Leah Brown, and Jen Weaver-Neist.

Finally, I would like to thank my family for all the support that it took to get this book done. My wife, Alicia Kersten, not only for the book writing, but for the two decades of very long work weeks that provided all of the experiences and research this book is based on. Without her help, support, and constant encouragement this book would not have been possible. Thanks also go to my children Tula Kersten and

Kaia Kersten for helping come up with many cover ideas. Finally, I would like to thank my parents, Greta and Gregory, and to my brother and sister, Marta and Mark, to whom I am grateful for all the big discussions over red wine in which they challenged the very foundation of every idea I've ever had.

— Metrics of the Value Stream

Flow Items
- Features
- Defects
- Risk
- Tech debt

- Value
- Cost
- Quality
- happiness

Business/ Methods/ Results

1 Flow → Distribution of ?
2 Flow Velocity
3 Flow time
4 Flow load
5 Flow efficiency

Flow metrics

— M+PS — must be on train

align around value vs. architecture Pg 160

Internal adaption rate of market

$\frac{Pg 159 + Pg 160}{Pg}$ Thrashing ↑ as disconnects btw Arch + U.S.

Pg 199 bottlenecks in core platforms due to lack of funding

Are our managerial process stuck in the manufacturing age? Pg 206

ABOUT THE AUTHOR

Dr. Mik Kersten started his career as a Research Scientist at Xerox PARC where he created the first aspect-oriented development environment. He then pioneered the integration of development tools with Agile and DevOps as part of his Computer Science PhD at the University of British Columbia. Founding Tasktop out of that research, Mik has written over one million lines of open-source code that are still in use today, and he has brought seven successful open-source and commercial products to market.

Mik's experiences working with some of the largest digital transformations in the world has led him to identify the critical disconnect between business leaders and technologists. Since then, Mik has been working on creating new tools and a new framework for connecting software value stream networks and enabling the shift from project to product.

Mik lives with his family in Vancouver, Canada, and travels globally, sharing his vision for transforming how software is built.

(op involvement